A CAT IN MY LAP

Story and Poems
Jenny Melmoth

Illustrations
Jo Berriman

Jenny Melmoth is a southerner by birth
but adopted the North West some twenty years ago.
She is a performance poet, and creative writing tutor
with the Disabled Not Daft Writers Group.

Jo Berriman is a designer, illustrator and cat lover
who works from her home in the Peak District.
This is her first collaboration on a full length book.

Printed by Trafford Press, 418 Chester Road, Manchester M16 9HP

OTHER BOOKS BY THE SAME AUTHOR:

Tell You a Poem
St Boniface and the Little Fir Tree
*Feet First - Poems for Dance
*Footsteps - More Poems for Dance
* (co-written with Malcolm Brown)

A Cat in My Lap copyright © Jenny Melmoth 1997
Cover & all illustrations copyright © Clowder Books 1997
First published by Clowder Books 1997, PO Box 11, Macclesfield, SK10 1FQ
ISBN 0 9530472 0 2

A CIP catalogue record of this book is available from the British Library.

To protect people's privacy certain names in this book have been changed.

Acknowledgements

The author would like to express thanks to everyone who has helped to make this book possible. In particular for their help, encouragement and/or expertise: Carole Baldwin, Michael Bamford, Commonword, Hazel Densem, Irene Gigner, Verity Heap, Nicola Kurowski, Selwyn Russell Jones, Graham Melmoth, Joan Poulson, Brian Redman, Jaz Singh, Ron Smethurst, Barbara Ward, Pat & David White.
Special thanks to Jo Berriman.

The author wishes to acknowledge the use for reference of a BBC publication CATS - The Rise of the Cat by Roger Tabor. Thanks are also due for permission from Faber and Faber to quote an extract from 'The Wasteland' by T.S.Eliot - Collected Poems 1909-1962, and from Aitken and Stone to quote from Jennie, copyright Paul Gallico 1950.

'Not in the Cat Show' has appeared at Scarborough Airings, in the anthology 'On Legs Made for Flying' and on BBC Radio Merseyside.

Contents

The Story

The Poems

A Cat in My Lap

No one can expect
my full attention
when there's a cat in my lap.

No one can expect
me to open the door
(even for another cat)
when there's a cat in my lap.

No one can expect
meals or tea or coffee
or me to answer the phone
or awkward questions
when there's a cat in my lap.

It is expected that
everyone will read the signs:
DO NOT DISTURB
(there's a cat in my lap).

For Graham

Chapter One

A New Home

The cherry trees were in their November glory as we arrived. On either side of the path leading to the front door of our new home, they were poised like a *corps de ballet*, their branches a dazzle of pink and white stars. Dainty as dancers, they wore their winter costume as lightly as the frothiest tutu. They formed a welcome arch as we stepped from the car.

We needed that welcome, for moving out of 'Glenmore' the previous day had been bleak and sad.

****

We loved 'Glenmore'. Situated in an Essex village between Chelmsford and Bishop's Stortford, we had lived there for the nine years of our marriage. We had found it on a warm August afternoon in 1966; the typical country cottage, lathe and plaster painted white, with a pink pegged tile roof and roses round the door.

The day we took possession our two mums were with us to celebrate the occasion. It was the 9th of December, a grey, wet day with never a leaf, never mind a rose in sight. The tiny rooms stripped bare of furniture and pictures looked dismally grubby. The kitchen was especially interesting. It looked out over a grim privet hedge and a ditch that divided the garden in two. This ditch was now full of water, so that the kitchen, a shifty lean-to, had the feel of a house-boat afloat at high tide, with water just about to burst ankle deep through the damp boards that were already spongy to the touch.

Graham's mother who was always the eternal optimist, said nothing, but my mother, for whom Graham could never do wrong, had long suspected her elder daughter of being wildly impractical and of lacking a proper sense of impending gloom. As soon as she had me to herself, she said, "You must have talked him into it. You can't go and live in that slum."

I had not talked him into it and we had no intention of living in a slum. The wedding day was to be 17th March, so we had time to effect changes. Graham moved in straight away to begin the task and like most new owners of a property was unimpressed with what our predecessors had achieved. He summed it up in a phrase which we often found ourselves repeating, "Never a screw where a nail will do." He moved in with a bed, a table, one chair and an empty whisky bottle which he filled with hot water at night for bedtime comfort. He took lessons in wallpapering, and I was there at the weekends, painting and sanding beams along with the best of them. So much so that it was nearly a case of "…and the bride wore an attractive volcanic eruption all along her forehead."

The dust from the beams came straight for the top of my head, hit my protective yellow headscarf and bounced grime into my forehead, where it raised an impressive array of bumps. Fortunately we only had two beams, and with generous applications of germolene to the stricken area the crisis was soon behind us.

It was a small village and we were conscious that our arrival would be watched and probably talked about, so just before the stroke of midnight I would be escorted next door to the thatched cottage of our welcoming neighbours, where I would chastely spend the night with a standard hot water bottle, thoughtfully placed in the cold sheets.

We were lucky to find a local builder who was just setting up on his own. He was pleased to remove the houseboat and replace it with a neat little kitchen in time for our return from honeymoon. The units were 'whitewood', solid but cheap. You painted the bare wood yourself, usually white, and spread fablon (in our case a pale yellow) on the top for the finished effect.

The weekend before we got married we moved our furniture and carpets in, and put up the curtains. There was a green Chinese rug for the sitting room and a deep blue for the dining room. The rugs measured 10ft by 8ft, and apart from the alcove in each room, they more or less covered the entire floor area. Our furniture was mainly Victorian. With my first earnings I had treated myself to a spoonback armchair which cost me £20. It still has the same upholstery, and along with the Chinese rugs all our furniture has stayed with us through the years. We were also very lucky in that my grandfather gave us some beautiful pieces, including an elegantly tall china cupboard that set off the alcove to perfection though it only cleared the ceiling by a whisker. All in all, as an acquaintance of my mother's said, for those G-Plan days, we had "funny taste."

We were pleased, proud and happy. The families visited on the Sunday, and this time even my mother was reassured, "It's a little palace." The only negative came from my grandmother who thought it was "very near the road." We laughed, but in retrospect she was right. There was a forsythia hedge and a rustic gate as protection, but even so, the distance from front door to tarmac was only seven or eight feet.

We now had each other, a house and a built-in dog whom I'd rescued from my social work days in Deptford. We'd changed his name from Prince to Tolly since it seemed a good match for Shandy, who was my parents' dog at the time. Tolly was reminiscent of a border collie with his black wavy coat, but his sharpish features were picked out in Chow brown. His legs and tummy were the same auburn shade and when he looked at you with his head on one side he was irresistible.

There was nonetheless a gap in our lives, or at least I thought there was. We could not begin married life or call it a proper home without a cat.

Chapter Two

Found

I need not have worried, fate and the village grapevine were an effective team. If it is true that when you go out to buy a cabbage you can meet either love or death, then it should be no surprise that going out to buy a lettuce is a good way to find a cat.

It was The Day of the Furniture, and I had been to do some shopping at the smallholding on the main road. On my way back down the lane, I met a friendly villager who quite rightly wanted to establish my credentials for carrying greengrocery past The Old Schoolhouse. Was I, she asked, the young couple who were moving in to Glenmore ? I admitted to being a guilty party, and she then told me some village history, quite a lot of her own family history, and that by the way she had three kittens and didn't I feel I needed one?

I said I thought we probably did, but what were they like?

"Two lovely tabbies, a boy and a girl but they're booked, I've only got the black one left. It's a boy."

Proving I was good at quick decisions, I said that if we agreed to have a kitten, we'd take the black one please, but I would have to check with my fiancé. In any case we would not be a legitimate home for about three weeks, as we had yet to marry and honeymoon.

Mrs Brayfield did not seem worried by the delay, as the kittens were only six weeks old. She said that she would be in all day if we wanted to view, adding as her parting shot, "But I'm sorry you can't have one of the tabbies, they're lovely."

Graham had already given a vague okay to the idea of having a cat sometime, but arranging to have a baby delivered immediately on return from honey-moon, was a shock, especially as at that stage he knew nothing about cats; his family had always had dogs. However, he instantly realised that my excitement boded the answer "Yes," and it was not too many minutes later before we were knocking on Mrs Brayfield's door. I had not mentioned to him that Mrs Brayfield seemed to regard "the black one" as odd man out, or maybe as the runt of the litter. I wondered secretly if we were going to be disappointed.

****

The door opened to reveal a steep mountain of stairs, with an intrepid little climber about half-way up. Each step looked big enough to require a rope and crampons, but he wasn't panicking. He looked down at us with blue-marble eyes framed in black fluffy velvet, as if to say, "I am sitting up here so that I can look you over properly. I think you might do. Come back in three weeks, and I'll give you a month's trial."

Graham was enchanted, Mrs Brayfield pleased by our reaction, and as for me, it was as well I had a wedding to think about, to take my mind off the excitement! We fixed the date that we would collect him and assured Mrs Brayfield yet again that we really did not mind about the tabbies. She found this hard, if not impossible to understand, but sweet as they were - and show me the kitten that is not - I had not felt the special rapport that was instantly struck with the fluffy mountaineer. Our kitten had chosen us.

We now had to choose a name. If you're lucky, once a name is selected and becomes a part of your cat, it's hard to remember how difficult it was to come to in the first place, but it can take many long hours of fun, frustration and ever sillier suggestions before you settle on something which is not only feline but suits your cat's particular character. Usually you are naming a kitten, so the hope is that he or she will grow into the name. There is always the danger however that the cat will grow away from its name, so that Titania becomes, in time, a solid Bagpuss of a cat and Hannibal produces kittens.

We must have had beginner's luck, as we found a name without realising how difficult it can be. We honeymooned on the Isles of Scilly, so were drawn to island names. We were able rapidly to discard St Mary's, and St Agnes, hovered a bit over Bryher and Tresco but felt that Samson was a gift. So 'Sam' it was, which hardly sounds original, but for us it had the satisfaction of relating to our honeymoon and being likely to suit our kitten's robust personality.

Chapter Three

Said the Cat to the Dog

We had arranged to collect Tolly from my parents in Beckenham, south east of London, on our return from honeymoon, and then to give him a day or two to settle in his new surroundings before the arrival of the kitten. We were anxious about this introduction; Sam would be so small and Tolly had a dog's normal tendency to chase cats.

Tolly thought he would like his new home until it came to bedtime. He had been used to sleeping downstairs in the kitchen with Shandy, my parents' dog. We therefore tucked him up, gently but firmly, in his familiar basket with his familiar bedding in the Glenmore kitchen, with plenty of reassurances about seeing him in the morning.

We had hardly reached the top of the steep narrow stairs before the frantic whining began. We ignored it stoically for a full minute before I went down to offer comfort. After this he was quiet for a while, well, long enough for me to get undressed and into bed. I got up and went down to him again, and then again. On the fourth movement of this virtuoso performance there was an explosion of rage from the lefthand side of the bed as Graham stomped resolutely out of the room, "This is ridiculous. Bloody dog. I'll sort him out."

I was alarmed. Had I married a secret dog beater? I lay very still and heard a stern, "Now then," from down below. Then all was quiet, too quiet. Next there was a shuffling on the stairs and a figure appeared in the doorway carrying a very large dog basket. "It's no good darling," said the figure, "He's getting himself in an awful state. He'll have to sleep with us just for tonight." The basket slid under the dressing table and Tolly with it, where he slept contented and quiet, that night and every night.

****

It was Sunday afternoon when Sam arrived and I had given the introduction of cat to dog much thought. I have always believed it important to effect introductions between animals carefully, making sure no one feels cornered or threatened by the other, and giving due deference to the well-established member or members of the family.

We walked with Tolly down to Mrs Brayfield, so that he should feel part of the welcoming committee, and Graham waited with him on the doorstep while Sam was installed in our neighbour's cat basket. He had grown as only a kitten can in three weeks, but he was still blue-eyed, fluffy and not very popular with his tabby brother and sister. Mrs Brayfield said she did hope we would not find him "dirty" as he wouldn't use the tray like the other two. We carried our rebellious outcast home, talking to him soothingly through the wicker of the basket, Tolly trotting on his lead turning a quizzical lift of his head toward the strange but tiny stirrings and mewings above him.

Once home, we kept Tolly on the lead, and lifted Sam out of the basket and onto the working top so that he should have the advantage of height if not size. He looked down at Tolly with resolute contempt, arched his tiny back and spat forcibly. The dog, twelve times his size, was immediately cowed and hid behind us for protection.

Sam was as cuddly, amusing and graceful as I had hoped.

He soon made it clear that he was not in the least "dirty" he merely wished to have his own private arrangements. He seemed well satisfied with the services rendered at Glenmore, and set about exploring the house and terrifying the dog by spitting at him any time he came within the proverbial distance.

We shut Sam in the kitchen that first night with a tray, and a cardboard box blanketed for the purpose, and he, the brave, the black and the silent, made not a sound till morning, though he romped ferociously on the bed chasing our toes under the covers while we tried to drink our early morning tea. We had a cat.

****

That same day, Monday, Graham returned to work, leaving me feeling somewhat post-bridal, as I faced a large pile of washing, and an antiquated single tub washing machine that did not rinse (or wash) very well. I had to heave the wet washing into the sink to rinse it and then into a recalcitrant spin-dryer. No matter how nicely you talked to this machine it remained bad-tempered at being asked to come out from under its working top. It performed furious pirouettes around the kitchen, spewing water defiantly as it went. The water went everywhere, but everywhere, except into the bucket with which I desperately chased it. Is this what married life is all about? I wondered. I never did get any better at doing the washing under this system, failing totally to build meaningful relationships with the machinery, so that Graham became used to wearing mildly grey shirts ill-matched by the gentlemanly white stiffness of the collars that were returned by the laundryman each Friday.

On this first Monday morning, Sam had wisely slept through the début of the Glenmore Washing Ensemble, nor did I ask him to accompany Tolly and me when we escaped to the fields and the ditches brimming with the fragrance of primroses. I picked some and placed them in little jugs round the house. They were patches of sunshine just as the rain started and the storm clouds brewed.

It was an impressive display - striking the telegraph pole only fifty yards from the cottage, with a bolt from the blackened sky. I rather enjoy thunderstorms but I had never experienced one quite that close. As the excitement built it seemed wise to seek the safety of the centre of the house as far away from any windows as we could manage. This meant perching halfway up the stairs. Sam by this time was not only awake but just a little disconcerted by the flashing and crashing around us. He snuggled into my shoulder and forgot to spit at Tolly who was cuddled against my legs with his quivering head in my lap.

As the storm abated, Sam realised that we'd all been in it together and he and Tolly tentatively touched noses. From then on they were good friends and Tolly ceased to be frightened of him, though of course Sam was always top cat. A bond of affection developed between them and the interaction between animals seems a good enough justification for having more than one.

Chapter Four

Home and Away

S am was tolerant of any visiting dogs, for being a sensible cat he took the view that if they didn't bother him, he wouldn't bother them. He was, however, as he grew up very much a 'family only' cat, usually disappearing if we had visitors, barely glancing in for meals, but appearing and chirruping rapturously, "Thank goodness they've gone," the moment the guests' car left the drive.

Even as a kitten Sam took life in his stride and we experienced very few crises. I demand fed him but he wasn't greedy - just a growing lad who needed plenty of loving attention. He never suffered from the nervous tummy sometimes displayed by kittens on being uprooted to a strange place. He showed every sign of finding his new home satisfactory, and we felt honoured to have been accepted so early on.

Nonetheless, one evening after about ten days, we lost him. It was a warm April evening and the door into the garden had been open for a short while, though I did not think Sam had gone out. I had been introducing him to outdoors slowly, and he had taken to the pleasures of tree rushing and twig chasing with abundant enthusiasm. At this stage however, his outings were still, in theory, being lovingly monitored. Graham had just come in, supper was ready, we were hungry, but where was Sam?

I discovered then something which has remained true despite being a pet owner for many years. There is little else that can invade me with more distress or panic than the unexplained disappearance of one of my animals.

We hunted the house through, and I searched the garden, using what was to become a familiar call to our neighbours, "Samsamsamsamsamsams..a..a...m, Samsamsamsamsamsams..a..a..m." No kitten.

The people opposite were in their huge vegetable garden where everything grew in luxuriant but rigid rows. Good country folk that they were, they clearly thought I was dotty to be even mildly anxious about anything as trivial as the absence of a cat. But it was *Sam* and he was so small, and *anything* could have happened; my imagination had begun to ruin my appetite. Nonetheless Graham was still hungry, so it was decided to abandon the search until after supper. As I pulled back my chair from under the dining table which was well draped in pink linen, a small furry person scarcely stirred enough to say, "Silly aren't you?" before returning to his slumber.

Sam never did come first call - it would have been undignified. I have heard people describe their cats as "obedient" because they come when called. Cats are many things, but obedient? Never. In my experience if and when they come it's because it suits them. Maybe they think there's a culinary treat, or an affectionate and warm night in from the cold, maybe they're just curious to know why you could possibly think it necessary to disturb their busy schedule, or maybe they feel sorry for you after a while, but I'm sure it's never because they think they have a duty to come, or that you might be displeased if they do not respond.

Sam usually came; eventually, quite rightly calculating that I would take it as a great favour and compliment that he should choose to do so. In those early days we did not have a cat flap, but would leave the kitchen window ajar for the cat if he did not appear. However, even then we preferred to close the window, especially in cold or wet weather, so would try calling him in for milk and biscuits before we went to bed. Hence my high-pitched call became a familiar feature of village nightlife.

****

There was a great deal still to do in the cottage and especially in the garden, much neglected by our predecessors. We knew very little about gardening then, but enough to purchase a doughty little Swedish lawn mower that would whirr merrily into long grass. It had much in common with the Ewbank carpet sweeper - light, easy and effective to use, with no need of cables or noisy engines.

Sam took to gardening. It was his favourite joint pursuit, helping by chasing the ends of weeds as they were pulled, or sitting, observing, offering supportive encouragement either close by or at a supervisory distance.

He and Graham developed 'Glenmore Golf'. This was played at dusk with an inverted walking stick and small fir cones that fell from our solitary pine tree. Graham, with surprising accuracy for one who reckons never to have connected any bat or racket with any ball, would swipe a cone into the adjacent field, and Sam would roar after it with all the speed and attack of a cheetah. He was not, of course, a retrieving cheetah, so an important part of the game was to select the next victim and then wait until Sam had strolled nonchalantly back into the garden ready for another 'kill'.

Haiku (on being called)

Not now, I'm busy.
Message received; might drop by
later - if inclined.

He also enjoyed going for walks, sometimes following us right round the field at the back of the house. The first time he did this, was after we had collected him from kennels where we had placed him for a few days when he was about five months old. I had not felt confident enough to leave him on his own at home. He forgot to be offended with us for abandoning him, he was so ecstatic to be back. He danced with us into the field and all round Tolly. I vowed then never to put him in kennels again, but always felt guilty leaving him on his own. He would punish us by ignoring our return for at least two hours, after which he would, at last, allow his feelings to show in rapturous greeting and silly kitten skitterings of pleasure.

If we were going away to parents or friends for a weekend we often took Sam with us. He was a good car traveller so long as he was not in a cat basket. Sam hated cat baskets. He could not see the need for them as I quickly discovered by his vehement vocals on the one occasion we tried it in the car. Once released from the basket he sat contented on my lap and from then on he always travelled on my knee. I enjoyed his purring warmth, for usually he was not a lap cat, more of a happy-to-be-alongside cat, so that he would come into the room, chirrup a greeting and then select a chair on which to keep us company.

Having given me the treat of the week by gracing my knee with his presence in the car, he would, on arrival at his temporary home where he was a guest, take it over with all the majesty of a visiting head of state, politely approving all the arrangements made in his honour.

Chapter Five

Disaster

The half-grown is a dangerous time for the young cat, the time when they are big enough to venture but do not have the maturity to cope with the dangers of the bigger world.

The accident that happened to Sam when he was about six months old was our fault. We had not taken proper account of his vulnerability. He was sensible, brave, companionable and full of fun. We thought it was enchanting that he liked to go for a good night walk with Graham and Tolly along the lane. The dog was on his lead, but Sam would skip along behind, in front, hide under hedges and then pounce out at Tolly's bemused nose.

On this autumn evening, however, a car came fast along the lane. Sam was drawn to the lights, ran towards them, was hit and lay still.

I was in the kitchen making drinks so did not experience the shock of seeing the accident happen, but I remember Graham's voice calling from the front door, and sounding more shaky than I'd ever known it, "Darling, Sam's been run over."

Of course, in that second before I saw him I assumed the worst, but Sam was now conscious and there was no blood, but he could not walk and was plainly in bad shock, from which cats can die. I tried to give him some warm milk which was a stupid thing to do, for had he needed surgery an empty stomach would have been necessary to give him an anaesthetic.

He was not interested in the milk anyway. I phoned the vet who said he would be waiting at the surgery, and we set out with the patient wrapped in a blanket on my knee uttering the occasional yowl of pain.

Our car was a faithful and ageing green mini. Graham drove with care because of the urgent yet delicate nature of the mission, but about halfway there we were stopped by a zealous policeman who had his suspicions about minis near midnight on winding country lanes.

"Do you realise your right nearside rear light's not working sir? " said the policeman intense with duty.

"Oh really officer, is that all. I've got a badly injured cat in here and we're *trying* to get to the vet," responded Graham testily.

"Oh dear, sir, I'm sorry to hear that." The attitude changed so rapidly to sympathetic concern, that I almost expected the offer of a police escort, with sirens and blue flashing lights.

The vet was standing by for our arrival, and he was reasonably reassuring. He gave an injection to combat the shock, said he thought there was no internal bleeding but suspected a fractured pelvis and would need to take X-rays. He told us to ring at eight-thirty in the morning.

It was a long night.

****

The telephone is a multifaceted character. It can be a lifeline friend if you need a doctor or to convey an urgent message, an intrusive boor if you are having a cosy evening, feeling private, or wanting to watch the one television programme of the week that you enjoy.

When you have to make the sort of call I had to make that Monday morning, the telephone glowers in the corner like a threat, and you wish it would transmogrify into a crystal ball into which you could peer for reassurance, without you having to lift the receiver and dial for the answer. However, I am of the school that if you have something difficult or unpleasant to do the quicker you tackle it the better; delay can only make it worse. On the other hand . . . while you don't know the bad news for sure, there is always hope.

I had this sort of conversation with myself until the hour came, and then stopped shillyshallying and dialled on the dot of eight-thirty. The news was moderately good - Sam would survive, he had no internal injuries but his pelvis was broken and he must be made to rest for at least two weeks.

At this stage I did not drive, but my kind next-door neighbour took me in her car, to be handed a bundle of very dispirited fur, but at least he was coming home.

When you buy an old cottage with the original village bakehouse in the garden, it can be surprising what gets left behind in it. Besides a rather nastily upholstered Victorian chair and a marble topped washstand (which after twenty-six years still graces the spare bedroom) there was an old parrot cage.

Well, at least the bell-shaped top part, about eighteen inches in diameter. I had no compunction about robbing my incompetent and unfriendly washing machine of its outer lid, which, upturned and with newspaper and blankets spread on it made a perfect base. This entire scientifically constructed recovery bay was installed on the oak chest in the back hall, opposite the open kitchen door, so that the patient would have constant company.

I was pleased with this convalescent accommodation, but nervous of introducing it to Sam. What would he think? He might be instantly resentful of such restrictions on his movements and lifestyle. Sam, however, was a sensible cat who accepted instantly that he was not well, and that he needed rest, if he moved too suddenly it would bring a tormented yowl. He was contented in his parrot cage, though far from being his usual cheerful self. We moved him as little as we could. It was possible to open the rusty door and put his food and milk in beside him, and I would remove the parrot cage and lift him down to his tray about every six hours which seemed to be enough, especially as he found this procedure very painful. I slipped some liquid paraffin into his food to keep his insides motoring extra smoothly, so as to cause him as little distress as possible.

I had, of course, rung Graham with great relief on Monday morning to tell him what the vet had said, but on Thursday he received what must be one of the strangest ever messages down an office telephone. I dialled excitedly to say, "Darling, *Sam purred!*" This was the moment when we knew for sure it was going to be all right.

When I took him back for his first check-up, the vet was amazed at how well the pelvis was healing and asked how I had been keeping him so still. Our resources of a clapped out old parrot cage and a common sense cat I suspect made veterinary history. We also had a clapped out old greenhouse in the garden, which had some good banks of earth in it, so that as Sam grew stronger we could take him out there for toilet arrangements. Thus he could enjoy having a respectable scrabble, protected to some degree from the weather, and safe from the temptation of lurching off into the wider garden to attempt too much too soon.

He trusted me completely, so that giving him pills was never a problem. I just talked to him soothingly, tucked him under one arm, opened his mouth, and popped the pill in, which he duly swallowed. He fully recovered, had his 'little operation', which he took in his stride, and matured into being an essential member of the family. He was neither very interested in, nor jealous of, the boys when they were born. He mainly kept out of their way, but continued to spend a lot of time with me, and thus inevitably with them, in the garden. We would watch him, silent and in slow motion, stalking a bird or an intruding feline, moving so lightly he was a cat on the moon, gravity suspended.

Sam had been special from the start, but a bond was forged while he was so dependent on me that was never broken between us. The trust was mutual and he was to play an important part a year or so later when our first child arrived.

Chapter Six

Birth Day

The day our first son was born, was 11th October; a surprise and a Friday. I was due to begin ante-natal classes the next Monday, his projected date of birth being 6th December.

I had had dull stomach pain all through the Thursday night and had hardly slept. In the morning, Graham with his usual optimism and general disbelief in illness took Tolly for a brief run before heading for work saying, "I should stay in bed till half past ten if I were you."

At surgery time I went downstairs to our one telephone, a red one in the back hall by the kitchen. I was able to speak to the doctor who said that he would call later in the morning but that meanwhile I must rest. Our GPs were a husband and wife team who knew every family in their practice, and were particularly keen on obstetrics. I was in good hands.

I went back to bed where Sam, having breakfasted, joined me, curling comfortably against my left side, purring gently. We were sleeping in the spare bedroom at the back, with its open view of the fields and countryside, for didn't we still have eight weeks in hand to finish decorating the baby's room? That room, at the front of the house, in true cottage style led off our bedroom, and the decorating had thrown us and ours into such disarray that it had seemed easier to change our sleeping quarters for a while.

The doctor came soon after ten, shushed the dog with cheery authority, but accepted Sam as chief comforter. I was told that I could be going into premature labour and we must try to forestall this with absolute rest, so no more going downstairs, though I managed to squeeze permission for two quick telephone calls; one to Graham, and the other to alert our friendly and reliable neighbours.

They were the best sort you could have. Anne brought me some lunch about twelve thirty, and Margaret who lived next door the other side, collected Tolly later to take him for a run in Hatfield Forest. Sam continued to keep me and my pink mohair dressing gown close company.

Anne came in again to clear the lunch tray and to make me a cup of tea, also to check that I was all right, which I was, more or less, the pain still a dull ache. She left me to have a sleep just as 'Woman's Hour' was starting at two o'clock. A few minutes later I went into what I now know to have been hard labour. Waves of pain swept over me while the cosy voice of 'Woman's Hour' made soothing noises from the transistor radio at the bedside. You would not need medical letters after your name to know that I was in deep trouble. The pain was so powerful that I did not dare to try to reach the telephone. The doctor had, after all, forbidden the stairs in the morning when the pain was only a breeze. Now it was a hurricane with the threat of tornadoes to come. It did not seem a clever idea to move from the bed much less attempt stairs. There were, however, brief lulls in the storm, and during one of these I tottered to the front bedroom and perched on the edge of that bed, which was piled with the muddle that we always create when we're decorating. I peered desperately out of the window for a passing Samaritan. Anyone would do; friend, dog walker, total stranger, shopper at the post office. But, of course, no one needed to post a letter or purchase tasty cheese that afternoon, no one's dog wanted a walk. I must have experienced four or five more tornadoes (or were they torpedoes?) before the relief of sighting the grandmotherly figure of our neighbour opposite, come out to do a little work in the garden.

I only knew her to wave to and waved now in between gusts, emitting an apology for a cry for help, which did not sound very loud even to me. It was the best I could manage, but as useless as whispering to someone on the far side of the Grand Canyon, especially as we discovered later that the elderly neighbour was very near-sighted, and extremely deaf.

By this time, panic was not just rising but in danger of taking off into orbit. I struggled back to the spareroom bed where I swore at the kindly, useless voice of 'Woman's Hour', which was about to read the serial.

"You're talking to me, I can hear you, so why the heck can't you hear me when I talk to you, and why don't you take any damn notice ?" This seemed a perfectly reasonable question to me, but amazingly the voice still chatted on, ignoring my plight.

I burst into tears of self-pity and fear for the safety of my unborn baby. I was not thinking clearly at all and could have been in danger of risking the stairs to get to the telephone. As the latest torpedo of pain exploded through me my hand came into contact with the warm purring curl of Sam and the next moment there I was sitting on the window ledge in my pink dressing gown looking down disapprovingly at my writhing whimpering self, with her hand on the slumbering Sam:

"For goodness sake!" I said, "Pull yourself together. You may not have started the classes, but you've read some of the book, and what does it say? Yes, NEVER PANIC as it can do neither you nor your baby any good at all. Breathe through the crisis, keep calm and believe that all will be well, even though you don't know how. STOP PANICKING, stop it at once, do you hear?"

I then got back into my body, felt the reassurance of Sam, and began breathing deeply and steadily while thinking rationally. The safest place was the bed, and with any luck Margaret would be bringing Tolly back soon after three o'clock. At the very worst, Anne had said she would look in again around four. I thus convinced myself that all would be well if I kept calm, and this was made easier by Sam, who had decided that his role was simply to be there, and to purr me through the crisis until help came. His plan worked, though it felt as if it took its time. It was nearly half past three before Margaret returned, and being worried lest she woke me from my peaceful slumbering she was going to slip Tolly inside the door and then steal away. This time, however, I made the cry for help carry, and action rapidly followed: both the doctors, soon followed by a blue-flashing ride in an ambulance to the hospital eight miles away. Harry was born at ten past five and weighed four pounds two ounces.

The worst casualty was poor Graham, who arrived ten minutes after it was all over, wearing a white gown which was less pale than his face, in which the only colour came from the reds and yellows reflected from the brilliant bunch of dahlias he was clutching in front of him like a good luck charm against the shock. But then he had not had the cushion of Sam at his side all day.

Looking back over everyone who was involved, including the medical profession, only Sam had remained imperturbable throughout that day. He was simply there, an assurance of normality and affection, affirming with his purr that all would be well.

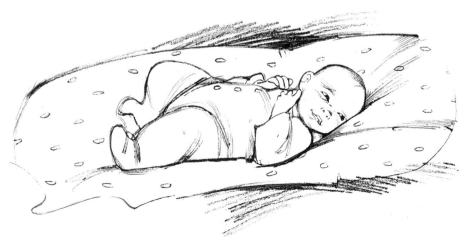

Chapter Seven

Of Plants and Flowers

Wednesday was library day. I would push the pram down to the main road where the van stopped outside The Black Horse, and would emerge after the allotted few minutes triumphant with such treasures as 'Dr Seuss' for Harry, and 'Down the Garden Path' for me.

Under the influence of books from Reads on Wheels, and my friends, Anne, and Mary (who had come to live next door but one), I became a keen though far from expert gardener.

While the children were very small and I was a non-driver, I was able to devote time to them while developing this new skill. Mums who are drivers always have somewhere to go, something to do, people to see. Life takes on a different, faster rhythm. I would not like to go back to being non-mobile, but at the same time I can understand why some people prefer never to get into the driver's seat.

Experts are necessary, but must also be taken with salt. The trouble with experts is that they are so keen on their own field (which is why they are experts) that they take it for granted that everyone else has that same devotion, whereas most of us only want to dabble. If you tried to follow expert advice to the letter, your early morning might consist of half an hour to put on your make-up, twenty minutes to do toning up exercises, ten minutes preparing your special muesli mix and counting calories, twenty minutes jogging, half an hour in the vegetable garden, maybe taking out a gentle trench for the potatoes, fifteen minutes grooming your Persian's impossibly long hair, half an hour extracting the essence of the day's news from the paper, not forgetting an hour of Open University, three pages of creative writing, twenty minutes meditation and a ten minute listen to the Teach Yourself Italian tape as you drive to the station for the 8.05.

I learnt a great deal about gardening from the books by Beverely Nichols because he made them fun, flowing with ideas into which you can dip, rather than stuffed with instructions to struggle to follow. Though some of his writing now seems unreadable, books like 'Merry Hall' and 'Down the Garden Path' are gems; funny and informative, ideas which now we take for granted, like putting white on white, or reds with clashing reds. 'Down the Garden Path' has been adopted as 'a minor classic' by the French, who are not only knowledgeable about cooking. Though I suppose it must be admitted that while they are also hot on language and good writing, gardening is not their strongest point.

Beverely Nichols loved cats as well as gardens. He always had two, his ambition being to own a hundred in his lifetime. They were called, with practical flair, 'One, Two, Three, Four' . . . and so on. I am not sure how near he got to scoring a century, but they often feature in the books. He, like me, never found them destructive, but then he, like me, had plenty of space. I suppose it is irritating in a small garden over which you have laboured much love, to find carefully nurtured seeds scrabbled up by a neighbour's cat, but then children also cause havoc by wanting to pick flowers for their mums, or as they become older, kicking footballs around.

Gardens are to be enjoyed, not just by plantsmen, but by everyone. The garden-proud mum or dad can be a pain. Many plants are robust. Choose these. If one or two stems get knocked or trampled, they will probably grow again, less damaged than the children's feelings if constantly shouted at or forbidden to use an obvious play space. Rosemary Verey who has a famous garden near Cirencester, did not attempt to create her marvellous plantings until her children were past needing to pedal their bikes over plenty of uninterrupted grass.

Children can be damaged by over zealous garden designers. A Sunday magazine once featured a garden redesigned by an expert. The "silly sandpit" was replaced by a pond (so much prettier) and the nasty muddy patch under the swing was replaced by sensible concrete (so much tidier and "look mum" no more muddy shoes). Now the intrepid six-year old falling off the swing would merely knock *himself* silly on the hard surface, and if that failed to quieten him down, there was a good chance he would stagger to the edge of the pond and still semi-conscious . . . drown. Plants meanwhile can suffer much more permanent damage from the hand that professes to love them than from the odd renegade ball or thoughtless trampling; the over-tidy gardener who drastically prunes back shrubs and herbaceous plants in autumn, instead of leaving them their straggly bits to protect them from harsh winds and frost, is a killer.

Cats enhance a garden by their graceful movements, the whisper of their feet on grass as they come to overlook your latest planting scheme, their ornamental flourishes up trees, and in the cool of evening, their twinky dancing on the lawn - stiff and quirky, then bursts of galloping chirrups with a sneak of the eyes to make sure you are applauding their display.

****

Flowers in some ways are like cats. Nestle your nose in the fur of a healthy cat and it has a fragrance worthy of a lily; try it in a lily and your nose will be painted an indelible gold. Flowers, like cats, should as far as possible be left to show their grace and charm in their own way, not made to "Stand up straight, and get your 'air cut you scruffy little soldier's button!" Similarly if we are talking cut flowers, they should not be over-arranged, primped and spiked and stuffed into unsuitable situations.

My award for The Daftest Flower Arranging Idea Ever goes to a scheme spotted in a smart magazine, for murdering tulips: "Take three dozen tulips and cut off their stems about half an inch from the flower heads. In a rectangular shallow dish arrange the flowers so that they form an attractive mat of colour."

In the accompanying photograph these poor molested flowers looked like a forlorn regiment of decapitated boiled eggs. The stem is surely part of a flower, and the way it 'moves' is a part of its character. Besides, not everyone can afford three dozen tulips as unwilling amputees. A little can go a very long way in the right container and setting. Five daffodils dotted among a background of green leaves, or twigs with catkins, can look stunning.

There are flower friendly containers. I remember my grandmother offering us an old, battered, and almost desilvered coffee pot which I accepted eagerly. Graham was nonplussed, and sounding like the princess in Aladdin said, "What on earth do you want that old thing for?" The genie that this elderly vessel hid was its ability to welcome flowers flung into it, making them look instantly happy. I would never part with it.

Similarly, my mother-in-law gave me a tiny copper kettle, profusely apologetic that it had no lid. I tucked an even tinier polythene container inside it to guard against leaks, and small flowers such as snowdrops, primroses, forget-me-nots or pansies look at home with minimal effort from me.

I like the container and the flowers to make their own chemistry of simple arrangement rather than following a set fashion of the moment, where every-body's flowers look the same because conforming arrangers have been to classes, and I'm yet to be convinced that flowers like being stuffed into squidgy oasis when they could be having a decent deep drink laced with sugar from a desilvered coffee pot or gritty pottery jug.

I am not above cheating by using walls and handy corners to help steady taller leaves, and there are a few tricks of the trade that are helpful. I have never gone to the Habitat extreme of taking a bunch of flowers and plonking them in a container like so many pick-a-sticks, with the tall ones at the front if that is how they happen into the vase, where they look uncared for and unloved. Flowers deserve treating with respect, so I have mixed feelings about what I do to tulips. If you pierce the stem with a pin about half an inch from the bloom it keeps them more upright, stopping them from taking a nose dive onto the table and they seem to last longer, so I don't think they mind.

Talking of tables, a posy ring is an easy way of creating a pretty centrepiece. I bought my pottery one for an olde tyme threepenny bit in a village jumble sale. It's ideal for little flowers, sometimes mixed with small pieces of foliage (often single leaves will do) or for broken-off heads of larger flowers - the small length of stem here is an advantage. I also have a glass bowl with favourite stones collected over several holidays. I keep them in water as they are more colourful when wet, and sometimes tuck in one or two flower heads among them.

I am afraid I have never been very good with indoor plants. I like the kind that bloom and can then be safely put in the garden. I reached the stage where I used to dread people bringing me plants for the house, as I would be sure to kill them, either by forgetting to look after them or by trying too hard. I think I have a slight phobia about indoor plants from seeing huge ones in other people's homes that I have felt were taking over, to the extent that they might gobble up the inhabitants in the night. Maybe the plants sense all this, which is why they give up on me, though there have been honourable exceptions like the lemon scented geranium which is so good-natured it has come to be known as the Sainted Geranium.

I am much happier looking after plants in the garden, and at Glenmore this was a rewarding task, partly because the soil was so good. True that the weeds wheeled at great speed but then so did everything else that enjoyed the fertile farmland of Essex. The wheat grew up to our back fence, and a sprinkling of cornflower or sweet william seeds produced miraculous drifts of colour not only the year they were planted but in subsequent seasons, for they would reseed themselves with enthusiasm.

Daffodils were farmed locally, so we were able to stock the more shrubby part of the garden with a sackful of these, which gave it a joyful dance of yellows each spring. The grubby looking privet hedge and the ditch met their end when Graham removed the one and piped the other so that it could be safely filled in. This seemed to make the garden look half as big again and certainly improved its image.

I was never an ambitious vegetable grower, but we had inherited a superb crown of champagne rhubarb and planted some fruit bushes. The vegetable area was only small so I concentrated on perpetual spinach and both French and runner beans.

We were both as green about gardening as you could be before the term came to mean environmentally friendly. It was a tricky moment that first year when I asked Graham to put up the sticks for the beans, and after half an hour went out to find a magnificent structure built with loving care and much string, perfectly positioned for the French beans, which had no intention of running anywhere. In my turn, I offered some rhubarb for the WI entry at the Essex Show and was chastened to learn that my well-intentioned trimming of the stems had rendered it useless for competition. It was such a comfort later that same summer to hear our neighbour's husband being chided for his help in weeding; John had succeeded in removing all Anne's precious strawberry plants.

No one can be good at everything, or if they are then they offend the rest of us who are no-hopers at a respectable number of skills. I began to build up some knowledge of garden plants, their likes and dislikes and their Latin names from books and observation. Graham knew a bluebell from a daisy and was content to leave it at that, but was happy to do the mowing, hedging and heavy digging, though the latter sometimes gave rise to problems, as the weekends when I needed it doing were sometimes a few months out of kilter with when he felt he could fit it in.

We got by, and I regard gardening as the art of the possible. It is well worth knowing your soil and conditions and hence the plants that are likely to succeed. You need a lot of time energy and resources to be a beater rather than a joiner. For example, we tried to grow a few heathers to keep the Glenmore pine tree company, but although we chose *Erica carnea* which is lime tolerant, they were never really happy. But some plants know our gardens much better than we do. Dainty columbines (aquilegia) grew with the enthusiasm of weeds under their Essex name of grannies' bonnets; unpretentious and pretty I much prefer them to their sophisticated overdressed cousins you meet at flower shows and in posh herbaceous borders. Sweet rocket or wild stock was another natural resident, and though rather gangly in habit it more than compensates for this by the softness of its white or scarcely pink, and its powerfully friendly fragrance.

It is also fortunate that plants do not read expert advice and are therefore capable of gainsaying it. According to the book, nasturtiums should be planted in a poor soil, otherwise they will produce an abundance of leaf with few flowers. Not these they didn't! Every year at Glenmore they would pop up to blow glorious scarlet and yellow trumpets of derision at the experts.

Sam was a very good gardener. He loved sitting near or watching sleepily from a distance to ensure that all was in order. Tolly liked gardening too, as it gave him the chance to slip away for an hour or two the moment your concentration faltered.

Chaper Eight

Enter a Puppy

I do not approve of dogs being loose on their own, and Tolly had a further fault, which was his dislike of any male dog on a lead. It was fine if the other dog were running free, and he had respect for 'ladies' at all times, moreover I do not think he ever actually mauled another animal, but he would bounce round growling and snarling in a manner sufficient to cover his owners in embarrassed confusion if we were there, and to worry them silly about what might be happening if he had gone off on his own.

We solved the problem by always keeping him on the lead near civilised dog-dom but taking him for an hour or so each day where we deemed it safe to let him run loose. After that he had to go on a long chain fixed to the apple tree, which kept him, us and other dogs secure. He did not seem to mind this, and would respond cheerfully when asked, "Do you want to go on your rope?"

Sam would often sit in the garden with him, looking thoughtful just beyond the length of chain. They were fond of each other and there was no doubt that Sam missed Tolly when he had to be put to sleep at the age of nine. His kidneys failed with nephritis, maybe a legacy from his Deptford days, and his loss affected all of us, except perhaps our younger son who was only a few months old. Sam spent more time close to us, whether to reassure us or himself I don't know, but it was very comforting.

We knew that we wanted another dog but felt that there should be a decent interval, partly as a mark of respect to Tolly. An animal is not a smashed plate to be readily replaced on the next trip into town. It can also be a mistake to replace before there has been proper grieving, for I have found you can half resent the new incumbent simply because they are not the old friend you miss. After all, if your partner dies it might be considered unusual to contact a dating agency the next day. On the other hand, although it is very painful to lose a pet I could never go along with the idea that that is sufficient reason for never having another.

The gap was a big one, the worst part being that going for a walk now seemed pointless. We had decided to wait three to four months, but barely made it past two and a half before I was ringing the vet to say that we needed to go out for walks and please could he look out for a suitable young bitch to take us. We had decided that life would be easier with the female of the species this time.

Next day we had a call to view, and Anne came to the rescue once more, driving me the ten miles to Harlow, while her daughter stayed with the boys.

The puppy was about three months old the vet said; a terrier cross. She was smooth coated, black and tan with a white chest. I thought she looked "very mongrelly." Anne thought she was "very pretty." I suppose I had been half hoping for a longer coated dog again (even now, a little resentful that this was not Tolly) but Anne was right and I was wrong. Anyway, if I had not taken her she might have been destroyed and I could not have lived with that on my conscience. We were warned that she'd been brought in for destruction because she had been "biting the children," but this proved to be no more than the normal nibbling by needles inflicted by all puppies while teething.

Choosing a name was easy. I had recently read a book about Alcibiades a 'Great Greek' who had a Persian flute-girl mistress called Timandra. I was so taken with the name that our second baby had been lucky to escape it by being born a boy. We called our puppy 'Timma' for short, and when Anne acquired a kitten a few months later he was given the glorious title of Alcibiades, known as 'Kiba'. It was something of a disappointment that no passionate romance ensued!

Timma was full of terrier energy, and unlike most puppies never seemed to need to sleep in the day. She could keep going endlessly until suddenly about seven in the evening she would crash out and not want to move again till morning. She was however, naturally good and well-behaved, in fact a timid Timma, so much so that at first Graham was not sure he was going to take to her. After Tolly she seemed "rather insipid." "Give her time," I said.

Sam glared at her from his worktop and majestically ignored her presence for the first twelve hours or so. Then on one of our puddle training trips into the garden he suddenly appeared from under a bush and began imposingly stalking her wherever she went. This speeded up till he seemed to be rather aggressively marshalling her around the garden, but always a few feet away. She thought it safer to pretend he was invisible, duly performed the puddle and came trotting in as if unaware of her shadowy pursuer. This exercise was repeated a couple of times and then Sam seemed satisfied that the newcomer was not a threat, but was going to be a permanent and suitable companion. They touched noses, Sam purred against her chest, and Timma decided like the rest of us that Sam was wonderful.

She rapidly became an indispensable member of the family, being called "Mumma" by our younger son, while I only qualified for "Nunny." She loved playing with the children and never showed any inclination to bite. In every way she was a success, but insipid she was not. She rapidly sussed Graham out, handling him with passive resistance, stubbornness and injured looks that had him obedient to her every whim.

In our turn we failed totally to persuade her to sit to order. She would stand quietly beside you, but however firmly you pushed her bottom to the floor it would never make contact. In the end we gave up. What did it matter? She was perfectly well-behaved, and never ran away, either from the garden or when out on walks, for though she would disappear for a while, rabbiting, she always seemed to know exactly where we were and would appear ahead of us laughing with the fun of being young, healthy and surging with energy.

She quickly got us trained. If you wanted her to come to you it was fatal to use a voice of command, she would merely look sulkily at you over her shoulder saying, "Don't you shout at me!" She taught us to speak to her in dulcet gently singing tones and would respond instantly to "T..i..m..m.a.. come on daaaarling." She shared Tolly's ability to distinguish between rabbits and squirrels (chaseable) and pheasants, chickens, sheep and other livestock (non-chaseable). She loved everyone including all other dogs, her own cat and any other cat she felt she knew as a friend. She had a particular gift for reassuring children who were nervous of dogs. By the end of their visit to us she had always helped them to overcome their fear and had become a firm friend and playmate.

The only disappointment was that she never did grow. We tend to like our dogs bigger rather than smaller, and we had been expecting her to reach small Labrador size, but she never made it beyond Manchester Terrier. Maybe she was older than the vet had thought when we took her home, but by the time we realised she was going to remain small and dainty, we were too fond of her for it to matter, contentedly referring to her as our 'Tiny Timma'.

Chapter Nine

Quit While You're Winning

Life at Glenmore was very happy. The village had a sense of community of which we felt part and to which we had always tried to contribute. There were unforgettable characters; old Johnnie, private as a mole in his dark clothing and rotting cottage, who rode a bike gripping a can of paraffin, and was too shy too speak, but would grin from under his squashed hat as he passed you on the road or as you passed his cottage where he worked the soil till he looked part of it, grimy yet earthsomely wholesome. He grew peonies which lined the path like blossoming courtiers, fit for royalty.

Then there were Horace and Phyllis who lived opposite the Old Mill, in a two-up two-down where nine children had been raised. You could hear Phyllis's "HALLO!" bellowed from her front door while we were still a quarter of a mile away. She would watch for us with fresh eggs or vegetables from the garden, which was prolific. Horace had handled horses and ploughing on the farm, and kept his steady hand. It was Horace who sewed our spareroom curtains for us on a machine dating from the Romans, and also made us rag rugs for the boys' bedrooms. Phyllis cut up old coats, old anythings, into the required strips, and Horace threaded them through hessian with skill and patience.

In the summer of 1975 there was great village commitment to support the church repair programme. There was to be a grand fête and open day, and people's skills were called upon. There were knitters and sewers and stuffers of cuddly toys. I am so good with a needle that I only have to look at one and the intended piece of cotton ties itself in knots of protestation before I have gone anywhere near it. But I am not shy about banging on doors if the cause is right, so I had a wonderful time ferreting the far reaches of the village for scraps of its history as reflected in photographs which could be mounted in an exhibition.

Ernie and Eva Brown were a brother and sister who lived in one of the white-painted bungalows on the little council cul-de-sac. Ernie was a gentle old man who tended the garden and grew vegetables on the small allotment opposite his home. Hugo still in a pushchair, would look forward to going their way as Ernie would give him peas, tender and sweet straight from the pod. Eva had a reputation for being a bit of a tartar, but she seemed to take to me, and lent me a photograph taken at the village school with all the other children when she was about ten. She told me that at the age of fourteen she had been sent off into service in Manchester: all alone on a great steam train, arriving in the pouring rain. The next morning she was woken by a loud roaring noise. Terrified, thinking it was some kind of gruesome monster outside, she got her courage together sufficiently to go to the attic window, where she saw hundreds of people teaming to their work in the mills. The cacophony that had alarmed her was the sound of clogs on cobbles.

****

Graham was also much involved in the exhibition, and had become chairman of the conservation society. We loved this little piece of Essex and its people. Our immediate neighbours were our good friends and we set up a cosy evening once a month which we called 'MASH' (Music At Somebody's Home). We took it in turns to play a programme of our own favourites; a kind of 'Desert Island Discs' without the interviewer but often with a cat on the scene, for cats love music. It made you listen to things which otherwise you might never have come across, for there was a wide range; from opera to oratorio to brass bands to jazz to pop. Some of us made exciting discoveries, though it could also be torture. This was part of the fun however, and you could always look forward to the coffee and the chat that came afterwards. I remember particularly an evening at William and Mary's, in their beautiful large old timbered drawing room, friendly with firelight. It was Anne's turn, but at that stage she and John did not have a suitable device for playing records, nor, said Anne, did she have enough records to make her evening, so with due apologies she had borrowed William and Mary's hospitality and some music from her teenage son. I was sitting on the floor or I might have fallen off my chair with enchanted surprise when some chords began which took me back to listening to Schubert's 'Trout' for the first time at school. The accompaniment was so much more than that, it enhanced the meaning of the words, which on their own would have been beautiful. Simon and Garfunkel were at their peak, and I was an admirer of theirs, but this voice was warmer, more approachable. Anne played the whole of the second side of "not till tomorrow" by Ralph McTell, and his music has been a comfort and delight to me ever since.

****

In many ways we had all we needed. We had always felt we had the best of both worlds, for while our own cottage was peg-tiled, on either side of us we could enjoy thatched roofs as pretty as any in Essex, without the anxiety that often goes with the picturesque. We had enlarged Glenmore while trying hard to preserve its character, and Sam had not registered any complaints once the six-month disruption of builders was over. He enjoyed the facility of the catflap which came with the house extension, and there had only been one other major trauma since his accident. It was one Sunday when returning from a weekend with parents, that he disapppeared. He'd travelled happily on my lap having enjoyed his weekend away, and I let him out onto the drive as soon as we were home while I concentrated on the children and unpacking. I thought no more about it until he had failed to appear for supper by bedtime, and was not there for breakfast.

I was then frantic, and went hunting and calling, imagining a mangled black body in a hedgerow. This mission failed, so on my return, even though I knew with my head there could be no possibility of him being shut in the bakehouse, I unlocked the door, peered into the gloom and emitted a faint "S..a..m.." I was greeted by an ecstatic mew and much purring. At which point I did what I always do in like circumstances; cuddle the lost sheep and burst into tears of relief. This has remained a mysterious facet of their mother to our sons as they have grown older.

"What are you crying for *now* mum, when everything's all right?"

****

We were never sure how Sam came to be locked in the bakehouse, but I suppose it goes to show that when anyone or anything goes missing, it is worth checking the obvious before scrabbling around in the undergrowth of the unusual. Another useful tip for finding things, given me by a friend and much practised ever since is, "If you think you know where something ought to be and it's not there - go back and check again." This works; well seven times out of ten it does. An important piece of paper may have got caught up between a pile of others and it is in that safe drawer all the time, your car keys are in your coat but you have put them in a different pocket, one you hardly knew you had, or they have slipped through a sudden hole in the lining of your handbag. Sometimes you have to send someone else to check the place where you have already searched six times. They then return, putridly smug, saying, "It was staring you in the face." You almost wish they had not found it. What sweet triumph though, when the roles are reversed and you are the one wearing the smile!

There are other occasions when things disappear for months on end and then quite suddenly pop up again exactly where they ought to be. This happens to me with earrings and T-shirts. So don't wear yourself out hunting, play the waiting game. We have to do this with the *Radio Times* which takes on very strange properties in our household. We can always find next week's and last week's copies but never this week's; until that is, it has become last week's, then there it is, bright as a disc jockey beaming at us from the magazine rack.

Socks have an embarrassingly high divorce rate. They go into the washing machine happily married, but only one of them comes out, the other having apparently left home, often forever. Scissors are slippery so and sos, but there is a way to deal with their disappearing tendencies. It's extravagant but it works. You have to have so many pairs around the house that they must compete for your attention, "Use me I'm the sharpest . . ." "No, use me I'm better at paper . . ." "Hey don't forget I'm great at knotty fur . . ." They are so stabbingly jealous of one another that they will forget about playing hide-and-seek with you and be meekly to hand whenever you need a pair.

****

However, there are more serious decisions to be made in life than how to out-wit your scissors. One such moment was fast approaching. To live in a country cottage with roses round the door is lovely, so is village life, but commuting to London can be a killer. Moreover, driving ten miles for the nearest shopping centre or swimming pool is not much fun for either mother or children.

When Harry had reached the age to go to playgroup I decided that I must con-quer my nervousness about driving. I had passed my test some years before, but had not driven since. Graham now had an automatic car, and there was an old aerodrome about a mile away on which he let me loose. About a month later, I ran him to the station for the first time, leaving him to worry all the way to work whether his wife, two children and dog had made the return journey safely. Slowly I grew braver, and began to look forward to the days I had the car. Eventually we acquired our first second car. It was a blue Fiat 500, the only car I have ever really loved.

It felt like driving a sewing machine only noisier, and you had to double declutch when changing down. Needless to say I had not the faintest idea what this meant, but unlike many a husband, mine said, "Look, if you try to do what I've just explained, you'll get in a muddle. Just drive it, ignore the weird noises, and gradually you'll get the feel of what you have to do." So I drove round for the first few weeks grinding the gears and alarming passengers and passers by, until suddenly I got the hang of it and felt I could call myself a proper driver.

We all loved that little car, and Hugo who was only about two at the time, could recognise a Fiat 500 at a distant glance, and regardless of the colour, would shout, "Little *Blue* Car!"

Graham had changed jobs twice since we had been married. The first move had taken him away from his relatively easy drive to the North Circular Road, and onto a train into central London. This was bearable, but the next job change meant travelling to the Waterloo Road, so the journey pattern was: car to station, BR train to Seven Sisters, tube to the Bank, a gurgle down The Drain, tube to Waterloo, walk to the office. This took an hour and a half on a good day, with no delays, strikes or staff shortages. The job itself when he eventually got there was demanding and I began to wonder if I was married to a man or a ghost.

It was taking its toll, so when the next job move was sighted on the horizon we decided that staying in Glenmore could no longer be a priority. If it meant moving house to improve the quality of family life, then so be it.

"What would you think about moving to Manchester?" he said one evening.

"Fine, okay," I said, feeling with my heart that I did not want to leave our familiar setting, yet somehow knowing with both my head and my intuition that, "The time has come . . ."

Chapter Ten

Go North Young Man

It was a good summer and the day in June that Graham was going to have his interview dawned warm and sunny. We left home early in the morning, parents, children and Timma. I had the usual lurch of conscience driving away leaving Sam resentfully flicking his tail where he sat on the drive. We were going straight on to Wales for our holiday after we had been to Manchester, so Sam would be cared for, well cared for, by the combined team of Mary and Anne (now working fulltime). But oh how I hated leaving him alone. We had considered having another cat to keep him company, but felt he was used to being King of the Patch and would resent any newcomer. This may or may not have been true given Sam's particular personality, but at this stage I still believed in the myth created in my mind by Rudyard Kipling of "The Cat That Walked By Himself . . . walking by his wild lone." Kipling has quite a lot to answer for; good writer and story teller he may have been, but he certainly misled me on feline sociology. All the cats I have ever known need and love company, whether human, or that of other animals.

****

Our journey north that Thursday is hard to reconcile to two intelligent, moderately well-travelled people one of whom had completed her studies as far afield as Dundee and Newcastle. Perhaps we had had up to date maps for all our previously successfully accomplished journeys round the UK and France. If so, it was a pity we did not have the same for the road to Manchester as it ran in 1975.

We set off sharp at six-thirty, along what my grandmother would have approved as "the pretty route" which took us down a lane that was single track at its widest points, and thence splashing through a dappled ford in the delightful Hertfordshire village of Braughing. Next, we wound our way stealthily through the countryside and when the M1 was not looking, snuck on to it.

There was nothing on the motorway to indicate that it was not continuing all the way to Manchester, but our antique map knew better. Cunningly, we deserted the M1 after a few miles to take to the secret byways again until our map said it was safe to return. By this ingenious method we managed to prolong a less-than-three-hour journey into five and a half hours. Add on the time for two good stops for children and dog, and you have Graham scraping into the building for his interview with about two minutes to spare.

As we drew nearer to Manchester so we were aware of dark cloud overhead and the temperature dropping. It was every southerner's cliché come true. "Do you know, we left lovely rural Essex in glorious sunshine but as we got nearer to Manchester the skies darkened and it poured with rain." Well, yes, I am afraid it did.

There was worse to come, for I had expected to find a pleasant city park where the boys could slide and swing in the sunshine while the interview took place, but it transpired that such areas are in short supply near Victoria Station and Corporation Street, besides, it was raining very heavily. The best diversion I could manage was to tempt the children to a bus stop with the promise of a ride on the top deck. I have no idea where we went, except that it was there and back, and was not the scenic route. This novelty trip served its purpose however, as the boys were suitably fascinated by wobbling around above the Manchester streets and it filled the necessary hour or so before Graham was due back.

We drove through heavy rain and heavier traffic out of Manchester on the A6 through Stockport and Hazel Grove, where we were slowed to a dreary crawl. I still hate driving on that road; if you take the inside lane you will be blocked by a parked car, and if you risk the outside lane you will be blocked by traffic wanting to turn right. It was unlucky that we were hitting this dazzling challenge at four o'clock, which felt like peak rush hour, and that it was part of my first impression of Manchester. It left me quietly praying that Graham would not get the job, as the thought of living anywhere near this damp, dreary, car-infested urban sprawl, filled me with dread.

We headed for somewhere called Disley and the Moorside Hotel, and then the clouds began to lift. It was green and open and the dog was made welcome in what the boys called the "helltel." They were thrilled as it had the space of long wide corridors which felt luxurious after the long confined hours in the car. It was also the first time they had had a hotel room to themselves with their own telly. We left them to the excitement of their enormous accommodation and a room service supper, while we indulged ourselves in the restaurant.

Next morning the sun came out, a little gingerly, and we took a brief look at one or two places on the south side of Manchester within commuting distance. I felt at least partially reassured by what we saw, so we were able to go on holiday to Wales feeling that if the job came up we could cope.

****

When it did, it was a wrench to sell Glenmore and to say goodbye to the village and all our friends. We felt we had become part of the community and people seemed genuinely sad to hear we were going. I refused to sell to anyone I did not like, or to anyone who had made rude remarks about the house, as a prelude no doubt, to seeking a price reduction. It was our home and we loved it, so only someone else who was going to love it should have it. I was determined to find people who would fit into the village as we had always tried to do. The agent thought it a very odd approach, but the market was relatively buoyant then, though country properties in the South East were being adversely affected by the first of the oil crises. Meanwhile, property in the North West was holding its value, so our supposition that we would be able to buy a bigger and better house for less money was wildly inaccurate.

Nonetheless, given the vagaries of housemarkets we were lucky. We sold Glenmore in less than three weeks and then spent a serious weekend house-hunting. We stayed in Alderley Edge with a widowed friend of my in-laws. Marianne was a person of some consequence locally and knew the area intimately. She was self-confident without being bossy, dressed elegantly and was cheerful and warm-hearted, always seeing the best in people. She would make positives of negatives, saying how lucky she had been to have all those happy years with her husband. She called everybody "dear" and it was impossible not to be fond of her on sight.

Our route north this time was an improvement on our first effort, though just through Newark I passed Graham a cup of coffee at the wrong moment and he spilt it all down his clean trousers. So far as I remember he drove all the way to Whaley Bridge, where we stopped for proper refreshment, in his underpants and a rather pink thigh, while the trousers flapped out of the rear window to dry. Marianne, as she gave us coffee and home-made sponge in her immaculate but cosy kitchen that Friday evening, thought we still had the route wrong: "You should have come through Derby, dear."

'Derby Dear' has remained our affectionate family name for the county town of Derbyshire ever since.

We sat there with a great pile of 'maybes' which her son-in-law had very kindly sorted out for us. He was with one of the biggest estate agents in the North West. Marianne's help in sifting the pile was invaluable, for she usually knew the exact position of each property and would say, "Yes dear, it looks a nice house, but it's on a busy road," or, "Oh, no dear, the inter-city train runs almost through the kitchen on the hour."

Amongst the pile of houses was 'Throstles' Nest'. Even Marianne did not know exactly where it lay, which, given its tucked away position on a dead end lane, was hardly surprising, but she did say, "Oh, Macclesfield is lovely dear." She came with us that Saturday as we reckied quite a big area of east Cheshire, looking at one or two 'maybes' from outside, but anxiously awaiting our afternoon appointment. The blurb sounded too good to be true. I knew there had to be a snag. There must be an evil smelling factory next door, or the intention of motorway past the garden gate.

I held my breath as we turned off the big main road and wound our way round a smaller one past a primary school, and then onto a lane that was more bump than surface. It took us past a large and beautiful pool with ducks and a swan, while cows grazed thoughtfully among chestnut trees, and the hills rose up behind like a composition for a painting.

We parked the car and walked the last stretch, along the narrow lane where I could see the white paint of eaves peeping above the trees and the charm of tall chimneys. There was no factory or motorway, and the house inside had all we needed. My face apparently gave far too much away, but then I think people like their homes to be liked, not criticised by potential buyers.

For a moment I wondered if I was getting carried away, but when Marianne sat down at the kitchen table and said, "Well dear, I could live here . . ." that clinched it for both of us.

We had drawn up a list of requirements for our future home before we started the hunt, and Throstles' Nest fulfilled all but one. It was within twenty miles of Manchester, had all the amenities of town, it was old and stonebuilt, as typical of the North West as Glenmore was of Essex, while all the extending had been done, giving us the exact accommodation required. True, the workmanship was not what we had been used to, and of course there would be things we would want to change, but overall it was as good as we were ever likely to get, given the unlooked for bonus that it was in the country, the garden backing into the hills of the Peak District with nothing between us and Buxton as the boot walks. The house was tucked away from the tiny lane within a tangle of trees and shrubs. Our fond relations might have their qualms about us moving to the Wodelands of Cheshire but at least no one could say we were going to be "very near the road" this time. Throstles' Nest would be a safe haven for cats.

This was given emphasis a few days before we moved, at a time when I needed positive reinforcement for uprooting ourselves. I was driving the Little Blue Car back from Bishop's Stortford about nine in the evening. I was coming through Hatfield Heath, descending the fast wide hill out of the village when a feline shape hurled itself at the nearside wing of the car. It was a suicidal cat behaving much as Sam had done eight years before.

I stopped, turned the car and was able to park in a side road with the lights shining across the main road to where I had expected the animal to be, but it had not been thrown back onto the nearside verge. Instead, it was lying in the middle of the road, vulnerable to the cars fast approaching up the hill.

If not already dead, the cat soon would be, squashed beyond recognition. So I jumped up and down in front of the body waving my arms clad in their dark navy raincoat, vaguely hoping I would show up in my own headlights.

Fortunately, the oncoming traffic responded to this strange spectre, and I was able to retrieve the body, which proved to be still breathing. I had to knock on three doors before establishing the owner, whose brother-in-law was just leaving, with the muttered comment, "Sorry, but I'm going in the opposite direction from Harlow." So was I, but since the husband did not want his wife to see her pet as she would be too upset, and he must stay to break the news to her, and comfort her, I found myself volunteering for the run to the vet, alone with an injured cat who might recover consciousness and vent its distress at any moment.

The line between bravery and stupidity can be a fine one, and is maybe only decided by the outcome. In this case it was happy. The cat, a young female, who "never goes across the road," was only concussed, and I received a letter of thanks telling me she had made a full recovery. This was forwarded to me after we had moved.

Chapter Eleven

' "Right," said Fred...'

We had been told about professional removers: "Wonderful, no need to worry, just relax and let them get on with it. They'll have magic screwdrivers that can collapse your antique table in three seconds and put it together again in two shakes the other end... saw a man take a twelve foot wardrobe through a six inch window, no trouble at all. No, don't worry about a thing, there won't be a scratch... they cover absolutely everything with simply wonderful cuddly blankets. No, honestly, it won't hurt a bit, you could have a house-leaving party the night before with the pictures all still on the walls, the removal men wouldn't worry, they'll have you all packed up in no time, so long as they get their cups of tea, you *must* keep them supplied with those cups of tea."

Despite all the advice, Graham had perversely decided to have a whole month off between jobs, partly to unwind and partly to give us plenty of time together to effect the move. The first two weeks were spent clearing out and packing up. We felt if anything, overprepared, almost apologetic that the paragons of pantechnicons would have so little to do on the day itself.

The night before the move we went to bed feeling confident. We had spent the last two weeks packing up pictures, crating books and the children's toys, and carefully removing wall light fittings. Moreover, Joan who had helped in the house for years, was coming to help me pack up the kitchen, and to clean through each room thoroughly before we finally left. The two boys would be safely dispatched, Harry would go to school and Hugo to playgroup and then lunch with a friend, the plan being to leave Glenmore by four o'clock at the latest.

I knew Sam would take a markedly dim view of his home being invaded and dismantled, so moving day was largely planned around his safety and comfort. We had cleared the spare bedroom completely, except for the carpet that was staying behind, and the necessary tray for Sam. With profuse apologies he would be settled in this apartment after his breakfast, the door firmly closed with a large sign saying, "NO ENTRY, BEWARE CAT."

We felt we had thought of everything, but we might have done well to remember Graham's favourite motto found on a matchbox: "Confidence is that feeling you get just before you fall flat on your face."

****

The day arrived; cold, wet and blustery, which was a bad sign, for it would mean that sooner or later we would have to turn the central heating off. Despite the extension, despite higher and higher chimneys and fancy cowls, we had never resolved the problem of the boiler being blown out in clouds of disgusting oily black smoke if the wind was feeling spitefully macho. This was Essex remember, where there were few hedges to curb its temper as it stormed up over the fields.

However, all seemed set to go well; the cat and the children were in position and the first of the 'What-Ifs?' safely scotched when the large pantechnicon arrived promptly at half past eight, with Fred, Charlie and a third man who was, I think, probably Bill aboard. We had our removers.

"Mornin' guv'," said Fred, "See you're nearly packed up then, 'ave you out of 'ere one o'clock, easy."

"Easy," agreed Charlie.

"Right," said Fred, "Let's get started. 'ow about putting the kettle on luv'?"
If moving day had been mainly planned around Sam, then I knew that the rest had to be geared to the hourly cups of tea without which removal men's batteries run down.

"Thanks luv' - right, well no problem 'ere," said Fred.

And so they got started.

Part of the meticulous plan for the day was that as each room was cleared, Joan and I would move in with hoover, duster and optimum cleaning power. Thus by the end of the morning, the house would be empty and gleaming.

"Got a screwdriver guv'?" asked Probably Bill. "We'll need to ease off one or two things to get them out."

This surprised us, for much of the furniture was in the drawing room where there were French windows for smooth exit, and I had innocently supposed that the loading would start from that point. I had my first clue that the day might not be going to run to my plan, and that removers do not work room by room, but by how each piece of furniture will fit on the removal van. Fred, Charlie and Probably Bill were about to build a three dimensional jigsaw, using all our worldly possessions, and without any equipment of their own - they had arrived with no hammer, no screwdriver, and with far fewer blankets than I had been led to expect, none of which looked remotely cuddly.

They made up for all this with their breezy cheerfulness. At the second teabreak Fred said, " 'ave you out of 'ere one-thirty, easy, guv'."

"Easy," echoed Charlie.

By the third teabreak, Fred still cheerful despite the rain and lashing wind, said, " 'ave you out of 'ere two o'clock easy, guv'."

"Easy," re-echoed Charlie.

"By the way," said Fred, "It won't be us what unloads you tomorrer."

"No?" we said, apprehensive.

"No," said Fred, "See, it's my first day back today, been orf sick a few weeks - can't go nowhere overnight yet."

"No," said Charlie, " 'e musn't go nowhere overnight, not just yet 'e musn't, and we're part of 'is team you see, so that means we can't neivver."

"'sright," confirmed Probably Bill, "So it'll be a different team unloads you tomorrer, luv', but (seeing my face) don't worry, they'll look after you. You'll be all right."

"Oh, that's all right then," I said, with all the confidence of the blown-out boiler which had sulked itself to silence in the menacing wind which was now whirling coldly throughout the house, the house which Joan and I could not clean because not one room (except Sam's) was anywhere near empty.

It was twelve-thirty and Fred said, "Well guv', we're just goin' to 'ave a spot of dinner now, but don't worry, we'll 'ave you out of 'ere three o'clock, easy."

"Easy," said Charlie.

I was beginning to get a strong feeling that I did not like moving days. I had stupidly planned to make cheese sandwiches for lunch, resisting all kind offers from immediate neighbours. I was cold with spirits nose diving, so when the phone rang and it was the rather overpowering owner of The Old Rectory from further up the lane, insisting that we must go and have some soup in her kitchen, I was not reluctant to be done good to. It was home-made carrot soup, piping hot in a warm kitchen. It was the best thing that happened to us the whole of that painful day.

Soon after this sanity saving break, we returned to the battle and a phone call to say that our younger son was becoming fretful; so he was brought back home. But home was now hardly what he was used to. Another Samaritan rushed in; Bridget, who had moved in next door where Margaret had formerly lived. Hugo devotedly referred to her by a corruption of her surname, "Fozdik." Fozdik, blonde and jolly, swept him up in a warmth of tea and telly until we could be ready for him.

By half past three, Fred was looking just a little glum, and said, "You know guv', they should 'ave given us annover van and a couple more fellers."

"Yer," said Charlie, "They should 'ave."

"Still, said Probably Bill, " 'ave you out of 'ere five o'clock, easy."

"Yer," said Charlie, "Maybe."

"Right," said Fred, " 'ow about anovver cup of tea, luv'?"

I was tired of making tea. Our elder son came off the school bus, was appalled by the unstately condition of home, and went to join his brother, care of Fozdik.

We were getting colder, hungrier and more depressed by the minute, especially as it began to get dark and there was only one 25 watt bulb left in each room, some of which were at last empty enough for us to begin cleaning. We could hardly see what we were doing, and anyway we had lost all momentum and enthusiasm. It was misery.

Finally, at six o'clock, Fred said, "Right then, well okay guv', that's it then. The new lads will be wiv you at two o'clock tomorrer."

"Thanks," I said, weakly, handing him explicit instructions and a sketch map to enable the new team to find the house.

They drove off into the darkness, and we took one last look at Glenmore. It no longer felt like home; cold and dark and empty, and only half as well cleaned as I had planned. Whereas earlier in the day I had been grieving about our departure, now I felt there was nothing left to do but go, and go quickly. The farewells were tearful but brief. Surely moving house was not meant to be like this.

****

I had, of course, remembered to give Sam his food, and he appeared calm and had contained himself rather than suffer the indignity of using the tray. We gathered the family into the car, Timma being the least bothered; so long as we were all there it would be all right. The only casualty of packing was the kitchen clock, an efficient wedding present of which we were fond. We forgot it, leaving it lonely on the empty kitchen wall. It was returned to us a few weeks later, but it had stopped, and although we gave it a battery transplant it never worked again. It must have died of a broken heart.

Could it have been worse? Of course it could. Many people want to move in immediately on completion at noon. Supposing our purchasers had been sitting out there with their removal van from half past one, as we should be doing tomorrow. It would have made a bad day unbearable.

As it was, we drove off into the darkness feeling like refugees. Graham and I were filthy dirty as well as cold and very hungry. My oldest trousers felt sad with grime, but Sam was on my lap, dear, imperturbable Sam, purring reassurance as usual, as we drove (avoiding the ford at Braughing) the hour's ride to the foot of the M1, and the anonymity of a motel at Hemel Hempstead. We had booked a family-with-pets-room, for we had anticipated our mood to the extent that a well-meant cheer you up evening with friends would not be what we needed. We did not want to have to be polite and cheerful and tell anecdotes about our removal experiences. Graham seemed more resilient than me; he was as tired, but maybe not as distressed by the day's events. My sense of adventure had deserted me, and I ached all over, inside and out. The children, understandably, were upset, and needed what comfort we could give them.

I have never been more glad to see a hotel, nor appreciated the motel system as much as I did that night. Graham checked in briefly, and then we were able to drive the car up to the very door of our room. As we did so, Sam, who had been saving more than his feelings up all day, could not do so any longer and a whoosh of warm liquid poured into my lap. He was only expressing what we all felt about Monday 17th November.

Chapter Twelve

Moving In

The "helltel" was heaven; in reality only standard for any establishment of its kind, for us it was five star. No one came near us. Sam and I sorted ourselves out in the bathroom. He had further comments to make but this time aimed them at his tray. I could do nothing till I felt clean again, so I stripped off, dealt with the grotty trousers, and then had the bath of the century. I emerged feeling at least half the woman I had been at seven o'clock that morning. The men just seemed pleased to be somewhere warm again where they could relax. We made a quick sortie to the cafeteria where we restored the inner person and then retreated to our sanctuary. Graham and I must have been asleep by eight thirty, "Easy."

The next morning the sun was shining and we could take our time to get on the road. We had promised not to arrive before one-thirty, so there was no pressure. Sam had spent a comfortable night on our bed, and Timma with the boys. We felt family solidarity could tackle anything. The drive to Macclesfield was uneventful, proving that the M1 linked into the M6 without any need for meanderings down country lanes. We paused for lunch, then drove on to our new home, in a mixture of excitement, sadness and apprehension.

I would have been warmly sympathetic if our predecessors had still been struggling to vacate the premises, but all was quiet and sunny. Throstles' Nest was waiting for us, the cherries welcoming us with their dancing displays of blossom. We had been told where to find the key, and there it was, sitting trustingly in the small garden shed.

We opened the front door and stepped into our new home, which did not feel like home - yet. We were guests in the house of the melting shadows who had lived here before. It seemed bigger than I had remembered, and the children ran all over it with the dog, exploring every room down to the large airing cupboard which could be used by small people and animals as a passageway beween the two bathrooms. Sam had a cursory look round, and then I made him secure in our bathroom before Removal Team Mark Two arrived at two o'clock.

I unpacked their tea things, explored the house some more, and waited. We waited some more. There are limits to how many useful things you can do in an empty house with no belongings. By two-thirty we were getting twitchy, by three o'clock becoming anxious, and by three-thirty we were sure that the van must be stuck irrevocably in the ford at Braughing. At four o'clock it trundled slowly into view, taking a branch or two from the trees as it did so.

"Sorry we're late darlin'," beamed Seán, "We lost our way."

"But, we left you a map… instructions…"

"Well, did you now… must have lost them. Still never mind we're here now, me and Michael."

"Just… the *two* of you…?"

"Oh yes, have you unloaded in no time, we'll be away by six o'clock, only of course, we don't know the load, so you'll have to help us… just a bit that is."

"Hallo Michael," I said faintly to our other remover, "I expect you'd like a cup of tea." He grinned disarmingly.

I had the feeling we'd been here before.

In theory, our darlin' boys were supposed to take all the tea-chests away with them, but even if Graham and I had scrabbled out the contents like starving dogs wildly searching their long lost bones, creating confused heaps over several floors, it would not have been possible, especially as we were also having to direct furniture to its resting places, and Seán did not have a screw-driver. He relented, saying we could keep any tea-chests we had not managed to empty, and then as darkness fell, soon after five o'clock, he summoned reinforcements, muttering, "Somebody underestimated this load, so they did."

By eight o'clock, Seán, Michael, Patrick and Seamus had worked nearly as hard as we felt we had, and with a last cup of tea and a reasonable tip to cheer their departing persons, we waved them goodbye, leaving us with a mere dozen unpacked packing cases.

****

Advice to cat owners is to keep your pet indoors for at least a week, preferably two, before allowing him or her to explore the new world after a move. Cats are said to be so territorial that some will make extraordinary journeys to return to what they consider home; not just a few miles, but distances such as from Glasgow back to Oxford. I knew all this, and about buttering the paws, yet somehow I had the feeling that any such fuss with Sam would be unnecessary.

We woke next morning in our bedroom with no curtains, to the sound of rain and Hugo's small voice wondering why there was water dripping on the floor by the end of his bed. He did not know about leaky roofs and we did not have much experience either. I began dank mutterings about paying £35,000 for a house that leaked, as I fetched a bucket to catch the drops. I was still feeling bruised by the leaving of Glenmore.

Sam, meanwhile, was making it very clear that he was only too pleased to have arrived, but was decidedly fed up with being shut in a series of prison cells, however comfortable. I opened the bathroom and the bedroom door, allowing him to resume his inspection of the house which he had begun the day before. Inevitably, with all the sorting out that was going on, and with our boys having already made the friendly acquaintance of the neighbours' children, doors got left open, and Sam began serious inspection of his new territory.

He was ecstatic, in fact it became obvious that he wondered why we had not come to live here before. It was a cat's paradise, with plenty of trees and under-growth to enjoy without any danger of a road. The little lane that ran past our house ended in a dry stone wall. There was a farm gate to the field to the left of it, and a footpath to the right, rising to the two small reservoirs to the south of us. The path was so steep in places for small boys' legs that we called it 'The Beanstalk'. The stone wall was shielded from the lane by a small patch of rough grass, measuring only about nine feet by eight. Its ownership has never been resolved, but it forms a semicircle where fishermen were tempted to park. This was a nuisance, as the turning space for our cars was tight, and it tended to depress the efforts of my newly planted daffodils to burst through and brighten spring days. We worked at it, ringing the green with stones so large as to qualify for rocks. Resolute fishermen would remove the rocks to park, and then, inevitably, fail to replace them. We persevered; we planted more bulbs including snowdrops, and in later years a larch tree, which we hoped would soon grow big enough to repel any attempts at parking. The grass was 'strimmed' once the bulbs were safely over, and this tiny area has become a valued focus for anyone coming up the lane.

We refer to it as 'Betsey Trotwood's Green', because I would get so unreasonably cross with any motorised lout who dared to defile 'my' green that I began to remind myself of David Copperfield's Aunt Betsey Trotwood, who was constantly enraged by donkeys being parked on the green outside her Dover house; she would cry "Janet, donkeys!" and then she and her maid would rush out to evict the animals and "the unlucky urchin in attendance who had dared to profane that hallowed ground." She won many a battle, but I am not sure if she ever won the war. We did. No one parks on that green now.

****

Sam helped Graham to put up the black cast iron lettering that spelt 'Throstles' Nest' on the white-painted porch. He strolled around the lawns looking lordly, and spent hours helping me to plant the hundreds of daffodil bulbs I had brought with me from Essex. It took nearly till Christmas and was fitted between floor staining and painting, and a thousand and one other new home jobs.

The most vital of these was to equip Sam with a proper doorway to outdoors. The previous owners had not had a cat, and the utility room had no outside door where we could make a flap. We were not keen to put one in the kitchen door as Timma, tiny as ever, could at a pinch have squeezed through it. Our vendors had recommended someone good for curtain making, who in turn recommended a carpenter, who not only recommended a good dentist but was also pleased to accept the challenge of constructing a cat ladder. The eventual system we concocted was elaborate: eight wooden steps up the outside wall leading to a comfortable platform outside the utility room window, six feet above ground level. From this platform the cat flap in the window was readily accessible to the inner window sill, with an easy descent onto a carefully placed wooden cabinet, thence to the floor and through a second flap into the kitchen. Sam found these arrangements fully satisfactory, and his new home and garden exactly what he had been looking for all these years.

****

We were doing our own settling in, helped by the friendliness of everyone in the neighbourhood. The boys had been whisked off on moving day itself to play with new friends, and within days all four sets of neighbours had made contact and invited us for a drink and made offers to help in any way we needed. Our small part of town felt like a mini village. Our arrival was made very easy for us. I gave vent to just one flood of tears on the second evening when I put the phone down after ringing Essex to say we had arrived safely, "I want to go home," I sobbed. Moving house not only upsets people but can play havoc with the finer feelings of your electrical equipment. Within a week, the iron, the hoover and the fridge had all decided that moving north was not for them and curled up their flexes on us forever. However, for the rest of us, including thank goodness my best friend the automatic washing machine,

Throstles' Nest and Macclesfield became home remarkably quickly.

I loved the narrow old streets of Macclesfield, where there were proper cobblers and saddlers and deeply old-fashioned ironmongers who would take trouble selling you two nails. I loved the old silk weavers' cottages with their extra storey where people used to work from home. Most of all I loved coming up the somewhat urban main road, turning off it, and watching the country landscape unfold, getting better and better as we neared our door. It gives me a thrill even now; that and the hills, and being close to so much wonderful scenery.

I liked having shops and swimming baths near the doorstep. I liked the Macclesfield accent and being called "loov." I became slightly embarrassed to say "barth" and "parth" in my hard southern tones. Some confusions arose, for example the boys had always spoken about "plimsolls" in relation to gym shoes. Up here they were called "pumps." They resolved this by talking about "plumps." Thus, in relation to a cat's coat, a bump or lump of fur is now referred to as a "blump."

****

We had been at Throstles' Nest only a few days but Harry had insisted on starting school that Friday morning. Escorted by Timma we walked merrily the five minutes along the lanes and past the pool, and left him happy enough in the care of his new teacher. Soon after, because Hazel (next-door but one) had kindly offered to look after Hugo, Graham and I went into town to choose light fittings.

We were successful in our purchases, and returned near lunch time to collect our younger son, who seemed fine, but it was one of the very few occasions when I have ever seen Hazel looking frazzled. She is usually calm in any storm, but to lose your neighbour's small son from your own kitchen must have been a nerve-breaking experience. One minute he had been happily playing with her own little boy, the next… he had evaporated.

She had, of course, checked to see if he had come home, but the house was locked up. Next she thought of going to the school to see if he had gone in search of his brother. She took her own child in the car and set off, happening to meet a police patrol car on the way. The police were instantly concerned and sent another car and a tracker dog to search the fields, the main anxiety being the danger of the reservoirs and the deep pool on the way to the school. No Hugo. No Hugo for quite a long time, till he suddenly appeared at the back-door of Throstles' Nest clutching his teddy bear. He had felt tired and wanted his own bed, had found the patio doors at the back of the house unlocked, opened them and carefully locked them behind him, and then simply gone upstairs to bed with his teddy.

Yes, he had heard and seen the policemen calling, but had been frightened, thinking he must have done something wrong, so only dared to appear when it had gone quiet again. It was all very logical to an almost four year old, but made poor Hazel literally ill with worry. Being her, however, it did not stop her having both the boys to play again and again. She and I found we had much in common and became firm friends, which undoubtedly was one of the reasons I settled so quickly.

We had been very lucky to fall into such a friendly little community, and it was not long before the only nightmares I ever had were that for some reason we had to leave Throstles' Nest and go back down south.

Chapter Thirteen

Inside, Out, and Front to Back

Whenever dreams of leaving Throstles' Nest occurred, no matter how jumbled they were, a constant feature was the stairway and landing. This had been the area of the house to make the deepest impression on me during our first visit; it is long and low and wanders on several levels with two bedrooms at one end of the house, and two more keeping the bathrooms company at the other. It evoked immediate, strong childhood memories of happy times spent with my grandparents in their house in Chislehurst, where I would snuggle in the vast featherbed safety of their spare-bedroom, which was along a landing that divided and wandered, guided by white balustrades. Having these memories so powerfully stirred, inevitably helped to make me feel I belonged in this house and that I would be happy living here.

We gave the boys the two rooms at the south end of the landing, overlooking Betsey Trotwood's Green and the rickety wooden structure known as the garage, while we took the bedroom-ensuite-with-popular-blue modern end. The landing knits the two areas of the house together spaciously and comfortably, though from the outside, particularly at the back, the effect is strange and higgledy piggledy. The various angles of the roof form a unique conglomeration which would not win any architectural prizes. If we had planned the extension we might have been less bold, creating something smaller, more pleasing to the outside eye but achieving less living space.

Anyway the die had been cast for us. It had been one of our stipulations when house-hunting that we did not want to build another extension; we had experienced it once with one small child, and had vowed that we would not suffer it again with two. Our predecessors had lived through the dust, the cold and the discomfort for us, and then moved on, leaving us to put our own mark on the house. I think everyone wants to do this in a new home no matter how perfect it may be when they move in, and to be candid Throstles' Nest was less than perfect. At Glenmore our predecessors had had a predisposition for nails rather than screws, in our new home they had thought on a larger scale, preferring it seemed, job lots; among these were radiators, blue basins, formica cupboards and probably builders!

The doors in the new part of the house, for example, appeared to be constructed of recycled egg boxes (almost before recycling had been invented). We considered these a poor substitute for the handmade pine doors we had left behind. The tiles on the dining room floor were black and white vinyl, which I hated, and the house was haunted with orange. It was a very large kitchen, glowing with formica which at first I found cheering, but coping with an orange bathroom suite as well, built none too slowly to a surfeit. However, this was the era of strong colour and we had left a fair smattering of purple to our successors at Glenmore.

It takes time to achieve all you want with a house. There is the initial burst of enthusiasm, and then the energy and the money start to run out. It can also be a mistake to make changes too quickly, particularly to an old house, where you need to absorb its character, lest you spoil overnight what has been there for centuries. However, certain changes at Throstles' Nest seemed to be pleading to happen:

The drawing room is under the boys' rooms in the oldest part of the house, and when we came, neither that room nor Hugo's above it had a window in the wall facing up towards the hill. It seems likely that these walls had been left eyeless because previous occupants had been more concerned about keeping warm than admiring the view. Our immediate predecessors would certainly have effected the change had they not been fully occupied with the extension.

A window specialist duly came, and I told him I wanted a window to match the mullioned one on the south wall, which alas, only looked into the seamy wooden side of the garage. Just as he was leaving, I caught sight of the sketch he had made, and saw to my bemusement that it was of a plain picture window. When I queried it, it was his turn to be bemused, for the measurements side to side, up and down, matched exactly, and it had not occurred to him that I could actually want a window with "dividing bars" which would "spoil the view" be "very disappointing" and worse still "more expensive." I managed to convince him, not that I was right aesthetically, but that I was the customer, dotty or not, and that this was what I wanted and was willing to pay for.

It was a salutary lesson in communication. How often do we base our interpretation of what someone else wants merely on our own experience and judgements? Conversely, how often is something so nose-bumpingly obvious that it does not even occur to us that anyone else could be thinking differently? Consequently, we do not state the obvious - sometimes with disastrous results.

****

The first year living with a garden is exciting, for you cannot be sure what treasures are buried. It is as well to wait until you know, before rushing to make drastic changes. Gardens, like houses, have their own ambience, and particularly if old, this takes a while to absorb, to appreciate, to savour.

The front garden was overplanted and overgrown, yet had a magical feel to it particularly at night, when lit by a tall white painted lamp which looked as if borrowed from 'Narnia'. I was anxious not to destroy this atmosphere.

The beautiful winter cherries were accompanied by the cotoneaster on the front wall of the house. It stayed in bright berry beyond Christmas, to be joined by a winter jasmine, and then snowdrops began to peep pale spears through the blank ground. In early February, they were spread, if not in a carpet, in rugs of white through the front garden, and as years went by I lifted a few clumps as they finished flowering and replanted them to create new rugs in previously unfurnished areas of the garden.

By early spring we knew that we must do some clearing, took a deep breath and began by removing the conifer in the middle of the larger lawn, replacing it with an elderly birdbath for which I advertised in the local post office. It arrived in separate pieces of dressed stone and had a mildly tipsy look when put together. The top section was hollowed out, but so shallow that Graham thought any self-respecting bird would deem it a paddling pool. Nonetheless it somehow looked right, has proved surprisingly popular with the birds, and takes far less light and space than the conifer.

Next we tackled a huge and peculiar holly with sinisterly twisted leaves which glowered threateningly at the kitchen window. We reduced this to a four foot stump, which in the obliging manner of stumps, sprouts sufficiently to be kept in neatish green trim. It has a compensatory moment of glory each Christmas Day when I rush out with the secateurs, garnering a single stem for the top of the pudding, and it gets a round of applause in a burning ring of brandy.

We had made our start, and then we watched and waited and watched again.

One of the best surprises came in April with the flowering of a shrub outside the smaller window on the south wall of the drawing room. As it came into bud, I registered properly that it was a daphne and that the deep pink colour of the buds exactly matched the colour of the velvet curtains which framed them, a colour chosen several months before in London. We received unde-served acclaim for the effect, people thinking we had designed our curtaining to our daphne. I wish we were that clever.

March and April were a triumph for the Essex daffodils which burst on the scene with fervent enthusiasm, especially when they discovered there was little or no competition from residents of the same species. They were particularly showy in the rough grass close to the field at the back of us, where I had planted the bulk of them.

May wore mists of many blues, as honesty, bluebells and forget-me-nots flowed across the sudden burgeoning of growth that this month always brings.

After the blues the colour began to fade. True there was a tangle of old lilacs and mock oranges which posed as a shrubbery and masked a narrow rose bed with venerable bushes that struggled in the shade, for the winter cherries formed leafy umbrellas through the summer. There were few late flowering shrubs, though an elderly deutzia made a valiant attempt and the small yellow and orange welsh poppies (*Meconopsis cambrica*) popped from everywhere; shade, stony path, solid rock. Another established garden resident, flowering in June and July was feverfew, with its quiet daisy flowers and bitter tasting leaves that are said to be good for headaches. There were two climbing roses, a pretty pink one that waved at Harry through his bedroom window, and a brave yellow that defied the colder climes near the landing window at the back. Foxgloves grew idiosyncratically in places which only they could choose. I have never succeeded in growing them from seed, and they resent being transplanted from whatever niche they have chosen for themselves. Some years they almost disappear, perhaps testing my affection, for I am certainly fonder of them when, after a calculated absence, they return with an army of friends the next summer!

Though in some ways our new garden resembled the one at Glenmore, having open fields behind it, and being wide rather than deep, it proved to be a horse of a very different fettle.

****

From our bedroom a rather crookedly fitted patio door led onto a balcony, which I swear had been built with a job lot of planks and thin tin floor, then suspended like an afterthought, using double-sided sticky tape and drawing pins. Nonetheless it was a pleasant vantage point. On still evenings you could hear the tinkling rush of water falling stream-like down the sloping stone overflow, from the top to the lower reservoir, and the view of the hill was an injection against any mood of depression. You could sometimes watch the moon make an entrance from behind the dark shape of the hill, rising with theatrical speed into the space of sky.

This was also an important place to do gardening, if you believe that they also garden who only "stand and stare." Our new neighbours to the back of us were two horses, a chestnut and a grey who came first to check that we were suitable and then to see whether we had good supplies of carrot. They were prevented from making forays into the garden by the beginnings of a beech hedge and a white ranch-style fence, which seemed appropriate for horses.

As the weeks ticked by, however, the minutes spent gardening on the balcony grew more extended. Something was fundamentally wrong with the design of the garden. It took a long time for me to spot the obvious, which was that the white fence was a barrier between garden and field. It chopped them artificially into two separate areas, whereas the natural lie of the land decreed that one should flow into the other. With a cry of "Eureka!" and a pot of green paint, the garden was transformed in a moment (well, a morning) by simply painting the fence away.

At Glenmore the field behind us had rolled into the distance more or less on a level with the garden, changing with the seasons; the dark of ploughed earth over the winter, the green of growing wheat, followed by its gold, and then the stubble, soon to smoke signals of a return to the plough. At Throstles' Nest the backdrop was always the green of pasture, and though the trees would give the game away, the seasonal changes that they made were also happening in the garden, so that the garden seemed part of the hill. Thus, it could never be formal. I had no ambitions to recreate here the island herbaceous beds I had left behind.

It was just as well, as this was the only lawn among the local households large enough to withstand football, cricket and the mysteriously complex game of 'Blocky Off' which no adult could ever fathom. We could not fathom the moles either, who were also fans of our lawn. I had brought euphorbias with me to plant as strategic weapons of repulsion, but the moles seemed to enjoy them and responded with encouraged flingings of earth. We then planted whirly windmills and whistling bottles, tried hosepipes of water, holly leaves, unpleasant smoky things, unpleasanter loud music, mowing four times a week, feline patrols . . . the moles thrived and invited distant relations to come and view our antics. Meanwhile the surface eruptions were only outpaced by the soggy unsafe feeling as you walked across the grass. At any moment your foot could lurch into underground city, wrenching an ankle as you went. For years I resisted calling the mole catcher, but in the end had to give in to Graham's entreaties. Hating it, I went out that morning.

****

There were other reasons why ambitious herbaceous projects would probably have failed. We had moved from rich agricultural soil to an acid earth at which many of my old friends turned up their roots. I found it very disappointing, for the list included, cornflowers, nasturtiums, hollyhocks, delphiniums and my beloved Mrs Sinkins pinks - dainty, frothy white with a heady perfume, they had travelled with my grandmother from Chislehurst to her garden in West Mersea, Essex. Their offspring had then merrily multiplied at Glenmore. They always reminded me of my grandmother with her taste for the cosy - anything louder than Cole Porter and she would switch the radio off in disgust saying, "Why can't they play pretty music?"

However, plants that like acid soil, heathers, azaleas and rhododendrons, of course did well, and there are others which have a sunny disposition and seem to settle nearly anywhere. I brought a few slips of santolina with me which rapidly formed a low feathery silver hedge. I was proud of this achievement until I almost destroyed it one year by tidying it up in the autumn, exposing it to some bitter January weather without the protection of its feathers. As I struggled to revive the remnants I took a vow against too much autumn pruning. The santolina and many other plants overwinter in a straggle of split ends, but respond with style as soon as they have their spring haircut.

Gradually I was going to have to learn, not to resent the disappointments experienced in this garden, but to work with and respect the fact that it has a strong will of its own. After all, it belongs to the hill.

Chapter Fourteen

Discoveries

The Little Blue Car was also learning about hills. Some of them she would tackle only in first gear, and even then sometimes I thought I would have to get out and push, but I coaxed her affectionately, while she muttered encouragement to herself. We always made it to the top, and it was always worth the effort as the boys and Timma and I explored the countryside, and the many interesting places which Derbyshire and Cheshire offer.

At weekends the bigger car came out to play and one of our jaunts was to Jodrell Bank, which is a good place to go to put your life into perspective, as you become awed by the size and complexity of the universe and impressed by your own insignificance. The planetarium was particularly enjoyable, and also faintly familiar, with a familiarity more recent than my teenage visit to the London appendage to Madame Tussaud. I was puzzled by the feeling until the next time I walked up the field behind the house. As I reached the middle, I realised that the skyline came round me like a goldfish bowl. The effect is exactly that of being in a planetarium, except that after dark, the lights from the town illuminate the western rim and the stars move rather more slowly than at Jodrell Bank. I am not convinced that our moon is much slower though, nor the rising sun, which on a good day pushes gold up above the hill before its bright disc appears. I suppose I ought to be an enthusiastic astronomer with all this on my doorstep, but alas, recognizing Orion's Belt and the North Star is all I am good for.

There was an evening, however, when I thought I was hallucinating. It was in June of the summer of 1976, that hot summer which turned the reservoirs to lidos, and the Cheshire hills to Assisi brown. Graham was already in bed, and I was about to undress when I thought I heard the sound of bagpipes. I looked up the hill and sure enough there was a lone piper skirling his heart out, complete with kilt. The sky was turning to dusk but he was held in sharp silhouette, and the effect was eerily enchanting. Graham was able to confirm that the strange musician was no figment of my imagination, but no one else apparently heard or saw him. He never appeared again, and we wondered if he was a ghost who only walked on that certain night of the year. If so, he must have laid himself to rest with his swan song, for we have never seen or heard him again, though I do not give up hope.

****

It was one Sunday morning in spring, well before the Night of the Piper, that I had gone with Timma to post a letter, and to have a small local explore. We had wandered along the canal to the main road, admiring the occasional narrow-boat which had emerged from hibernation, extrovert in its fresh plumage of red and green, ready to roam the man-made rivers and shoot the locks for the summer months. I decided to take a look at one or two of the roads near the canal on the way back. This was not popular with Timma as it meant being on her lead which she regarded as boring and undignified, unless the road was a busy one, when she welcomed the security of being attached to me.

The gardens were pretty in their spring outfits and I was noting how well maple trees flourish in Macclesfield, when my attention was seduced by the most beautiful cat I had ever seen. It had a long creamy coloured coat while the face, ears, tail and legs were meltingly delicious chocolate. The eyes were bowls of forget-me-nots.

I felt I could not approach any nearer to this magical creature with Timma in tow, as it might take fright and disappear, so we kept at a respectful distance, despite my desire for closer acquaintance. Fortunately someone was working in the garden next door to my target, so I plunged into the sort of conversation that always embarrassed my sons: "What a beautiful . . . whatever is . . .? Is it yo . . .? Would you happen to know who . . .?"

Ten minutes later I was excitedly telling Graham the glories of this wondrous feline, and within a week had rung the owner and been invited round to meet Monty properly. He was as friendly and cuddly as he was beautiful, playing endless pat ball with a rolled up piece of tin foil. He was a Colourpoint, though the Americans have the more romantic name of Himalayan. It is a breed evolved from Siamese being bred with Persian, so that the cats have the Persian shape and build, including rounder than round eyes, but their colouring and 'points' are Siamese. I was enchanted. "One day," I thought, "One day I shall have one of those."

Of course there was no question of having another cat at the moment. We would not have dreamt of upsetting Sam, moreover I was struck with other twinges of guilt, for I have never been an enthusiast of pedigrees and 'good breeding'. I can just about accept that once there may have been a case for breeding working dogs to fulfil specific functions, especially in the huntin' and shootin' field, but have been appalled by the overbreeding and inbreeding that has produced animals which cannot breathe properly (Bulldogs and Pekinese) with a predisposition to back trouble (Dachshunds) or to hip dysplasia (Alsatians and Labradors). It seems iniquitous to mutilate puppies by tail docking, or to manipulate animals' genes, for human profit, pleasure or ego massage, and it would be tragic to see what has happened to dogs overtake cats, though already some Persians are so flat faced that their noses have almost vanished.

Was I not in some way condoning all that by besottedly admiring a fine example of genetic engineering? Frailty thy name is me. The trouble is that I like beautiful things, whether it's a flower, a picture, a piece of furniture, pottery, Chinese carpet or a cat, though with pets the personality is an important part of that beauty, and Colourpoints tend to be gentle and affectionate. I salved my conscience by telling it that when the time came, any Colourpoint kitten we had would be balanced by a homeless moggy. For the moment, we had the one and only irreplaceable Sam.

****

Meanwhile, Hugo was settling well at playgroup and beginning to make friends. One day in May, William came to play, bringing his mum along with him. While she and I were strolling round the garden, I introduced her to Sam who was enjoying the newfound pleasure of a snooze in catmint, which was a plant he had not experienced in his previous surroundings. He looked up to greet us, and all she said was, "He looks sad."

I wished I had taken more note, and blamed myself afterwards that I had not taken him there and then for a check-up. By the time he was beginning to go off his food it was nearly July.

The vet said that Sam's kidneys were huge, and diagnosed nephritis. The word beat inside me like a cold drum, for Tolly had died of it. There was no cure. The vet advised a low protein diet of fish and chicken, and was able to give injections to help keep the inevitable at bay. At that time there were no specialised diets for kidney illness but I followed the vet's advice to the letter, and Sam, of course, was sensible and co-operative. That summer, famous for being one long heatwave, was perfect for enjoying quiet places in the garden, though as time went on, Sam seemed to require the deeper retreats of wardrobes and cupboards.

Over the next few weeks I was preparing to lose a best friend, and this was hard, especially as I knew that the ultimate decision of when we said goodbye would rest with me. I felt I had betrayed Sam by not realising sooner how ill he was, and trying to tempt him to eat unsuitable foods. Another good reason for having more than one cat, is that it is easier to sense when one of them is below par, for you can compare notes by watching and touching the others.

64

If you have never been close to an animal, then it is probably impossible to imagine the level of pain that it causes to lose one. You are losing a member of your family, a part of your everyday landscape, a piece of you, of all that is home. It can hurt more than losing some people.

I was nonetheless aware that to decline into the hollows of depression because of the impending death of a cat would puzzle the world, for it was not my husband, child or mother that was life-threatened. Somehow, out of the mixture of strong emotions and listening to favourite music, I found myself writing a poem. This was a surprise, especially as it was not a sad poem but a slightly silly one that helped to cheer me up. After this first one, came another and another till it became a habit, and I have been writing ever since.

Out of a dying
spilt a need,
out of the needing
sought a song,
out of the singing
solace spoke
as the first shy line
was born.

Chapter Fifteen

Death and Life

Once I knew how ill Sam was, I gave him all the time, care and love I could, and hoped that I would make the ending right for him. We went to the vet for injections several times over that wonderfully hot summer that I should have been enjoying more. The treatment gave temporary respite, improving his appetite and alleviating any discomfort, but through the picnics, walks and excursions to the Goyt Valley, Tegg's Nose Country Park and the Ladybower reservoirs, the threat of loss was always lurking.

It came one warm September Monday. The vet had warned me on our last visit two weeks before, that the next time Sam appeared to be going downhill, it would be kinder to allow him to do so peacefully.

We gardened that morning, Sam and Timma and I; gardened to gentle music that drifted under the cherry trees from the drawing room window. Timma and Sam were very fond of each other and I took a last photograph of them together. Sam had not been able to eat that morning, but was taking pleasure from his favourite occupation, safe with the person he most trusted. He was not yet suffering. It was time.

But the vet did not come. In a clash of duty I had promised to start regular sessions at Hugo's infant school this Monday, volunteering to mix paints and write names on paper. This was before I had known what the day would hold. Now it made an additional tension, not wanting the vet to come because of what it meant, yet needing him to come so that the ending could be as peaceful and unhurried as Sam deserved.

At half-past twelve the vet had still not arrived and I was due at the school by twenty past one. I rang the surgery and heard that he was on his way. I was hungry but not wanting to eat. I was struggling to force sufficient of a sandwich down to prevent my stomach growling at the children, when the vet came.

It was as I would have wanted it. I cradled Sam safe in the warmth of the garden sunshine, and there, purring in my arms, he left me.

I had thought that Timma ought to see him to say goodbye, but she had fled up the field and would not come near. She knew what had happened, what I had done. Does death have its own smell?

Gently I groomed him, wrapped him in a piece of blanket he was fond of, and laid him where he often used to sit, beneath the largest of the winter cherries. I marked the place with a white quartz stone, then resentfully stifled my tears under a pair of sunglasses and walked shakily round to the school to face sixty small children. They and the teachers must have found me very odd and withdrawn, but any attempt to explain would have reduced me to a soggy heap.

Graham and I comforted each other that evening, while the boys were much more matter of fact. There seemed no need to protect them from what had happened, for we were much more upset than they were. Maybe this is because death is a hard concept for the child's mind to grasp, but also because they had not known Sam from a kitten, and he had never been close to them as he had been to us, particularly to me. They did not like to see me upset, but otherwise they seemed to treat Sam's departure with an indifference that appeared callous.

****

For some of us, a house is not a home without a cat. When the home loses its cat it becomes incomplete, as if a familiar feature of a familiar painting went suddenly missing. Imagine looking at the ubiquitous Constable and seeing an empty river where the haywain ought to be, Van Gogh's 'Sunflowers' with one of the blooms tweaked away, or 'Whistler's Mother' with no lace cap.

It is unnerving and leaves an emptiness that is unbearable which you bear, you carry on living but you grieve, and you do not forget. It helped to know that the ending was as good as it could have been, and it helped to be able to prepare, to grieve in advance of the event; the healing came quicker but the absence lingered, so that after a mere month I knew I had to do something about it. It had to be a special something in honour of Sam; special but different.

****

We decided that this time we would have two kittens, one of my much admired Colourpoints, and a moggy who was in need of a home. I made a few inquiries about moggies but did not have any immediate success. The Colourpoint breeder on the other hand, had a litter who would soon be ready to go to their permanent homes. There was one male kitten available. We had decided to have males as I had been given to understand that they tend to have easier temperaments when doctored than females.

The kittens we were going to see were not Seal Point but Blue Point, which meant that their markings were a smoky blue rather than chocolate brown. I suppose this should have been a disappointment, but when we saw the kittens there was no question of quibbling. They were straight off a chocolate box, adorable and cuddly. It was the first time I had met someone who was part of the pedigree cat world or that I had been in a house that was devoted to breeding. Much of what Mrs Crawford said was jargon to me: talk of "queens" and "type" passed over me, I was just captivated by these little blue-eyed fluffs who would mature into long-haired blue-eyed seducers of the moggy-lover's heart.

'Kaiwon-Jorgi' was five weeks old and not a particularly "good" Colourpoint as he was too Siamese in "type" (shape). He looked all right to us, and he seemed to think my knee would do, so that was an easy decison taken. I asked how a Colourpoint might mix with a moggy and Mrs Crawford said that while there should not be any problem since Colourpoints have easy-going affectionate dispositions, she did just happen to have an older kitten from an earlier litter that she had kept back for possible breeding. She had now decided that he was not quite "good" enough, so would we like to see him? Graham and I looked at each other. We had the feeling that another decision was on the way.

'Kaiwon Marcellus' was of sturdier Persian build and looked huge after 'Jorgi', who had been put back to bed by this time, the litters being kept separate. His eyes were hugely round and his purr infinite. We exchanged smiles and Mrs Crawford offered £5 off the price if we took both kittens. If she had said she would add £5 to the total price for the two of them it would have made no difference. We had succumbed to the prospect of having these two enchanting creatures as part of home.

I asked what I hoped were all the right questions about the care of Colourpoints, and learnt that they were tough as any moggy but would arrive with their own diet sheet, a sample of which sounded like dinner at the Savoy. They would need toys and of course a comfortable box with soft bedding for their first week or two with us. To my question about where they would like to sleep as they grew older I drew the unequivocal answer, "On your bed."

We explained that we had planned a weekend in the Lake District in early November and would collect the kittens on our way home. The "boys" had never met as yet, but we were assured that they would get on as soon as they did meet up, and what better place for getting to know you, than the neutrally foreign territory of our cat basket.

****

Our own two boys were excited when they heard we were going to have two kittens, but appalled by our choice of names. This was unfair as we had thought long and hard, devoting days and nights to the decision. It can be hard enough to name one cat, but *two* who were arriving as a team ? A heavy task. We were seeking a male pairing of names, but went through everything from 'Pepper and Salt' to 'Jekyll and Hyde' to 'Gog and Magog' to 'Bubble and Squeak'. Nothing seemed to be quite right till Graham remembered our first date, when he had come by two tickets to Covent Garden for a performance that was noted for the quantities of tomato ketchup in the animal sacrifice scenes, causing a large gentleman in front of us to faint heavily into the aisle. I remember little about the music except that there was not a tune within earshot, but I do recall the restaurant afterwards, where Graham, being nervous of the unknown quantity he was dining, took a deep breath and with unerring aim exhaled it, blowing the considerable contents of the ashtray all over my side of the table, while clouds of volcanic ash rose to attack my crisp pink blouse. It was a performance worthy of opera, of Schoenberg, of 'Moses and Aaron'.

Chapter Sixteen

Meeting Points

Collection weekend involved some complex arrangements. Harry, Hugo and Timma were all staying with Hazel and her family, so their luggage went along the lane. The boot of our car boasted walking gear, a posh frock for dinner, and a cat basket, while at home awaited the kittens' layette and their Fortnum and Mason hamper.

I was nervous as only a new kitten owner can be when we arrived home, opened the basket and invited our new babies to begin exploring. It seemed a good idea to let them have a few minutes familiarising themselves quietly with the kitchen before the family returned in force. So we crept out of the house and went to collect our own species of boy. When we returned it did not take a genius to work out that we were fifty per cent short of our full kitten complement. Moses was delighted to see everyone and more than willing for a cuddle, but where was Aaron? Had Moses proved contrary to all knowledge of his breed, murdered and perhaps devoured him? For a long moment there were no clues, and then a pathetic mewing led us to discover Aaron, who had squeezed and then wedged himself into a one inch gap behind part of the working surface. Only Hugo had a hand small enough to reach in and rescue this original model for the helpless kitten. As he grew up we doubted if he were a cat at all. He was more like a lamb.

Like many cats, Sam had always given the impression that whatever he wanted, he knew you would eventually give him. He never sat looking wistful as a dog might do, but would purr round you, patiently confident that you would not let him down, and of course you never did for he made it feel a privilege to serve. If we had not been satisfactory I have no doubt that he would have moved on without so much as a second flick of his elegant tail.

The same could not be said for Aaron. All kittens are affectionate, but Aaron was ridiculous. While Moses would come and find you and leap up your back as if you were a convenient tree, Aaron could be heard plaintively mewing in the distance. I was alarmed by this at first, fearing there was something the matter with him. There was in a way - a need for constant cuddling. He is the only cat I have ever known who even when mature wanted to be picked up and fussed and carried about nearly all the time. He was also very chatty. In Siamese style he would hold conversations with me which made perfectly good sense to the two of us, if not to anybody else.

Having two kittens about the place was an infallible way of learning how to do things one-handed, for a hand was constantly needed to caress one kitten or the other. One kitten helping with the chores made them fun, two kittens helping made them hilariously slow, for every detail had to be investigated enjoyed and shared. Skidding between clean sheets and blankets was a winner at bed-changing time, taps dripping water would mesmerise for minutes, iron flexes had to be swung on and clean clothes sat on or hidden in, which did wonders for the crease factor. There were party games like 'Last-one-up-the-stairs-a-silly-billy'. This was invariably Aaron, appropriate to his soppy nature but also having to do with his legs being shorter than Moses' due to the age gap.

When the "boys" first arrived, I followed the breeder's advice to the last letter of their exotic menu. This, occurring three times a day, included raw minced steak, delicately diced rabbit and best white fish. Milk meanwhile had to be avoided as being "too rich." After three days of small smells and runny tummies I rang Mrs Crawford and we decided that they were suffering from "nervous stomach" as a result of changing homes. I persevered with various permutations on a theme of exotica till I concluded that the problem was as much one of overloading their small tums as of emotional upset. I did some experimenting of my own, cutting the meals back to two a day, trying tinned food and ultimately raw liver - which did the trick. It seemed to settle their stomachs straight away and they fed mainly on this for about two years much to the horror of the vet when he heard about it. Liver is very high in protein which is why cats love it. High protein is also why they become hooked on many of the tinned foods and those notorious "bickies." In theory I fed my cats wrongly for a long time, but like flowers who do not always react according to the book, they seemed to take no harm at all. I compounded my misdeeds by giving them milk, though they took the opportunity to drink water too, for Timma's bowl was always available.

****

Their tummies soon settled down and Moses and Aaron began to explore the wonders of the garden, games of hide-and-seek through the bushes, pouncing on the rustle of a fallen leaf, whizzing up and down trees, and the pleasure of claw sharpening on a particular lilac - the lilac Sam had also favoured. They selected this one trunk very early on and it has remained a favourite with all our cats ever since. Why? Is it the texture of lilac bark, the smell, or has this tree become imbued with belonging on Throstles' Nest territory?

As they grew, so did the length of their fur, and it soon became evident that their long fluffy coats were more than they could successfully manage either on their own or with help from each other. I tried grooming them, but this was not well received as they had developed a busy schedule, resented having their timetable broken into and probably found my inadequate handling of "blumps" uncomfortable.

Moggies like Sam can cope perfectly well with their own coats except when feeling poorly, but pedigrees of the Persian persuasion seem to be bred with ever longer coats that outgrow the capabilities of everyone but a show breeder or an international hair stylist. I had not been warned about this, and was somewhat ashamed to find we had two young cats who far from looking "long and lovely and lush" resembled knotty sheep ripe for a shearing contest. The solution was nearly as drastic; a trip to the vet and a general anaesthetic from which they emerged half shorn. They would have scored *"nul point"* for elegance, but several marks for their joyous break dancing as they tested the roll of fur on ground unimpeded by their tangled fleeces.

Slowly we improved our collective skills. I went for a grooming lesson and as a result invested in a cutting comb - thoroughly recommended even though it sliced my finger open as I struggled to extricate it from yards of protective sticky tape on arrival. Moses and Aaron also became more cooperative as they grew older; nonetheless it seemed an unnatural palaver of a way to have to treat cats.

They made up for this lapse in proper felineness by proving that they had hunting skills of feral ferocity. They formed a lethal team, sometimes bringing in two or three small corpses in a single day; mice, voles, shrews, but also a number of birds, particularly the young. It was heartbreaking to come down to a dead baby bluetit or to make vain attempts to rescue a fluttering throstle (thrush). The carnage that first summer was bad, with Moses and Aaron bursting with youthful energy and the need to try out their developing skills. Fortunately, with each year it grew less, and despite the cats' early predatory habits there were still plenty of garden birds till recent years, when for what-ever reason, we saw the triumph of the magpie set against the reduction in number of smaller varieties, thrushes becoming almost rare.

The worst aspect of cats hunting is what appears to be the deliberate torture of small creatures. They let the mouse run, then pounce on it, repeating the nasty procedure many times. I felt better about this after hearing it explained that cats do not have a jaw shaped to inflict a quick kill (as we had seen Timma do to a rabbit). Thus the cat is at risk of damage being inflicted on it by its prey. What we see as cruelty on the part of the cat, is nature's way of allowing the cat to tire the prey, making it less dangerous to go in for the kill. It also gives a sporting chance for the victim to escape. I was able to rescue several creatures who had scurried in temporary sanctuary under a bush, by removing the hunters from the scene and shutting them indoors for a while so that the mouse or shrew could make good its getaway.

The only mice we have ever had in the house, have been ones brought in as unwilling guests, and then lost to the crevices behind work surfaces. There was one morning when a fieldmouse was cornered behind a wellington boot, from where I thought I could rescue it if I removed Moses and Aaron. Just as I was securing number one hunter in the study, the phone rang, and I paused to answer it. When I emerged, there stood Dorothy (who had arrived to tackle our daily chaos) with her hand clapped placidly over one shoulder and Aaron sitting at her feet. "A blinking mouse has just run up my leg," she said as nonchalantly as if remarking that the post had arrived.

I was impressed. I am not afraid of mice, but the speed and suddenness of their movements make me jump and I would at least have uttered an "OOOH" of astonishment if I had been used as a vertical bolthole. I secured Aaron along with Moses in the study, then we walked to the top of the garden where Dorothy, like a Gulliver, lifted down her tiny Lilliputian passsenger who scampered off unharmed.

****

Moses and Aaron spent a great deal of time together. They would sleep in one chair wrapped round each other or squashed in a cardboard box hardly large enough for one of them. Often there would be a curl of cats on our bed round which we had to engineer our legs.

As they matured, they revealed the extent of the differences in their person-alities; both woven of the Colourpoint wool, one was warp the other weft. Aaron was the miaouing lamb wanting to be constantly picked up and cuddled. I could almost wear him round my neck like one of those deathly fox furs. He loved everything and everybody. He almost got me into trouble when we had some new friends to dinner. During the main course and under the secrecy of the tablecloth, the guest on my left experienced his knee being gently and fondly patted by his hostess. I had become aware of an anxious look invading his eyes but hadn't connected it with the person in my lap, till I rose at the end of the course, Aaron in hand, and the sexual harasser was revealed amid laughter and relief.

He was affectionate to the point of absurdity, and I remember commenting

Haiku (on beds)

You have made your bed,
now, I suppose to oblige,
I must lie in it.

more than once that you could have told Aaron till your face was several shades of dark blue about some people being unkind, and he would simply not have believed you. His world was one of comforts, fun, gentleness and affection. In this world cruelty to animals did not exist.

Nonetheless, I never saw him talking to strangers in the lane and he had a very limited territory, which appeared to consist only of our garden and the two immediately next door. He came instantly when I called him, whereas Moses in true feline style would "make a note for later" from his larger beat, which took in the gardens on the other side of the lane and some of the field to the back of us.

Moses was never spiteful but his affection for us was variable. Some days he wanted to be petted and stroked. At other times he would look at us as if we were notorious with the RSPCA and he would bustle off with unseemly haste, creeping close to the ground and casting anxious glances over his shoulder lest we should pounce on him. His relationship with Timma how- ever was unchanging. He would wind himself round her chest purring a devotion which was only outshone by his commitment to Aaron.

They were individuals with their own life styles and yet they were a partnership. They enjoyed what the boys called "silly fights" (they had them too) which gave every appearance of being fierce. The growlings and yowlings and kickings of white fur reached a level to alarm any visitor to the house, who would be confounded a moment later when the silent bell went at the end of the bout, and there they were placidly washing each other - even having a go at the uncomfortable "blumps", or merrily eating out of the same dish, though they had one each.

Moses and Aaron were as close as any two animals could be, and you would certainly have thought, "Three's a crowd."

Chapter Seventeen

Then There Were Three

Moses and Aaron had turned two years old, when one Monday in November, I took Hugo to school as usual to find a minor hiatus being caused by a white and black kitten. She was trying to get into the warmth of the school cloakroom, away from the cold snap of outdoors. Various mums were trying to shoosh her out, and the heavy door swung to on her slim form nearly squashing her and provoking a pained "Myick!" from the small refugee.

"She's very dirty," quoth a pristine person in a spotless pale blue anorak; the sort of garment that would have been assaulted with hairs and muddy dog in one swipe of the paw in our household.

"So might you be a bit grubby, if you'd been abandoned to fend for yourself when only half grown," I muttered to myself.

As usual, Timma was hitched to a handy litter bin a yard or two from the cloak-room door, so that I could see Hugo into school unencumbered. This left me free to talk to the grubby grey creature with the black splodges and the pink flower of a nose. She soon weighed me up as a hopeless softy, but I decided to make a brief test of her credentials for being a stray. I walked away from her. She followed. I unhooked Timma and walked with her well-mannered, by my side. She turned to look back at the small waif, who arched and spat venomously. By the time we reached the school gate she was still following us, so I capitulated, scooped her up and tucked her into the warmth of my jacket. From the safety of her cosy eyrie she was able to make contented purrings punctuated with warning hisses at Timma, who was looking faintly mystified by the unusual turn of our morning walk.

Moses was in the kitchen as we came in, and when he saw the intruder's head peering from inside my coat, he let out a growling howl, unlike any sound I had ever heard, but it boded menace, as if he would destroy this little lost moggy as soon as look at her.

From Moses' point of view, it was unreasonable to be bringing a stranger into his home without so much as a "Sorry, but do you mind?" I hoped that given time he would come round to the idea. Either that, or that the kitten would be claimed by distraught owners.

She was therefore made comfortable in Graham's study, given milk and food. It was only a little to start with, as I thought it best not to overload a starving stomach. My new friend disagreed. She gobbled as if she had not eaten for a week (which perhaps she hadn't) and then looked hopefully for more.

During that day I cuddled her on my knee whenever the big cats were safely out of the way. I was working on my first attempt at a villanelle (a set form of poem with repeating lines) and by three o'clock, with enthusiastic help from my unclaimed friend I had typed it up.

I then rang and left a message for Graham, who was at a meeting, that there was "a temporary visitor" in his study, "just till we find the owners." I was going out that evening before Graham was due in, so left the kitten on the chair, and the villanelle on his desk with a note which simply said, " What do you think?"

When I came back late that night I found the kitten still on his chair, and a response on the desk, "Delightful, and I like the poem as well. Why not call her 'Villanelle'?"

****

Thus 'Nelle' (pronounced 'Nellie') became part of the family. All efforts to find her previous owners proved futile, though after the head teacher had announced that a kitten had been found, a little girl came to look at her. I reacted to her rebuttal with mixed feelings; sorry that she had not found her own lost pet, but relieved that my new one was not to be wrenched away.

She came through her first medical check with reasonable colours, though needed worming, and later would have to be spayed. She seemed to enjoy her visit to the vet, purring in the basket as we travelled, and boasting to him how clever she was to have found a new home. While I was anxious for her to build up her strength, we had to find a sensible balance, for she behaved as if every meal was the last she would ever get, and had I let her, she would have eaten till she was sick. It took her a week or two to believe with all her plumper being that she would never go hungry again.

Nelle stayed in the study for three to four days, the big cats sniffing interestedly under the door, becoming I hoped, acclimatised to her presence. They showed no ruffled fur nor further tendencies to emit threatening noises. The moment of introduction came and went peacefully. Nelle merely walked out of the study, and with her back slightly arched approached Moses. With caution they sniffed noses and a mutual acceptance was struck. Aaron, as expected, was instantly affable, and we settled down to a *ménage à trois*.

****

Moses and Aaron remained very close, Nelle was on the outside of their relationship and they would occasionally gang up on her and chase her. She would spit and growl, her topaz eyes flashing flames. Minutes later she could be seen curled up on our bed near one or other of "the boys" though never wrapped round them, for Nelle was not a cat lover.

She had close rapport with Timma, with whom she could be found sleeping side by side on one of the big floor cushions. Sometimes she would greet us on our return from a walk up the hill, rubbing affectionately round Timma's chest. We wondered if there was some kind of pull between them by virtue of both being female. Certainly there were times when Nelle, Timma and I savoured being girls together in a predominantly male household.

It is said that neutered male cats have more affectionate easy-going temperaments than females who have been doctored, and in my experience I have found this to be broadly true, at least where other cats are concerned. Nelle could certainly be very ratty to Moses and Aaron, eventually commanding respect from both of them, secretly being fond of them, but not prepared to let it show.

On the other hand, she was very much my cat, and I could not have faulted her devotion. If I went out for a few hours it was always Nelle's tiny pink nose that came to greet me at the front door. If we were away, cat feeders would report that the cats had all been fine but that Nelle had looked utterly miserable all the time we were gone. Her health was never as robust as I would have liked, but she enjoyed visiting the vet, even being spayed did not put her off. The car journey never upset her and she seemed always to sense that I was trying to do my best for her.

The grubby grey of her coat quickly worked its way to polished white, with its randomly splashed splodges of black. She had dainty white feet on which she would go twinky dancing when the mood took her, madly skittering over the lawn and up into a tree where she would cast a glance to make sure we were enjoying the performance. She adored the sun, and would bask on the low wall near the side gate for hour upon hour in warm weather. She also showed some original tastes in food. She was mad on rice pudding, cheese, in fact anything milk based, but more surprisingly loved lemon cake. There is a favourite recipe which requires pouring pure lemon juice and sugar over the cake while hot and fresh from the oven, leaving the mixture to permeate for an hour or so before removing the lemonised confection from the tin. Before I learnt to take evasive action, I would return to find that the top of the cake had been raided, a sizeable crater of enjoyment nibbled from the sweet and sharp spongy surface. It seemed a shame to spoil her fun, but not everyone relishes Nellied cake, so we agreed on a compromise; I would share my slices with her.

There was just one occasion when Nelle gave deep cause for anxiety in her early days with us. She had settled so well, enjoyed her first Christmas and had at last become convinced that she would never go hungry again. Then she vanished. I was distraught.

****

She was not around at bedtime, which was most unusual, as she loved the ritual milk and bickies. It was a frosty night and I would have expected her to want to be curled up somewhere warm - like our bed. I called and called and then went to bed but could not sleep. I got up and pulled on wellies, warm coat and bobble hat, took a torch and went out calling again. Inside a minute Moses and Aaron had both appeared and padded round after me, their blue eyes glowing a surprising red in the torchlight. I walked round our garden, up and down the lane as far as Hazel's garden. I called and called, albeit not too loudly, bearing in mind that it was the early hours. I called and called some more, but still no Nelle, just Moses and Aaron who chirruped and skipped around me unsympathetic and unworried by my sense of loss. So much for cats' sensitivity to disaster. At last I gave up, went back to bed and slept fitfully until dawn.

I prayed that Nelle would be purring round the kitchen demanding breakfast, but was only greeted by the empty lurch in my own stomach on finding no sign of her. Moses and Aaron were irritatingly cheerful as they tucked into their food with their usual relish, while the boys and I got ready for walking to school. I came back with Hazel, who wondered if Nelle had been rebuilding her strength all these months ready to take off for new adventure. This sounded unlikely to me. I could not make it fit with the affectionate character of my little Nelle. I was convinced that something dreadful must have befallen her.

I walked back into the empty kitchen despondently, to hear a sudden booming crash emanating from the utility room. There was Nelle, grubby as the day I had found her.

It remained a mystery as to where she had been. If trapped behind the boiler surely she would have mewed. It seems more likely that for reasons of her own she had gone to sleep in the pleasant warmth, deciding she was much too comfortable to respond to my calling until hunger eventually stirred her. However, since she was never to disappear again and she had emerged as grimy as a trainee mechanic, maybe she had given herself a minor fright (although she did not look perturbed). Perhaps she had been perfectly happy until she wanted to emerge for breakfast, but then had to shove hard to produce the crash, her freedom, breakfast and the stupidly tearful reconciliation. She had, after all, been missing a full ten hours!

Moses and Aaron looked smug. They must have known all along. No wonder they were so amused by my torchlight searchings by bobble hat.

****

Nelle was a music lover. Fortunately she could combine this with one of her other favourite occupations: "keeping an eye on mum." She and I spent a great deal of time together in the kitchen, which was where I scribbled, crossed out, typed up and sorted out the endless mountains of admin: besides occasionally wafting an iron or peeling a potato.

Even with the aura of orange formica it was a satisfying kitchen. Measuring twenty feet by fourteen you could dance as well as eat in it. The window over the sink gave a leafy view of the front garden, and from the corner, where the pine table and benches sat, the window looked across the back lawn past a small ornamental crab apple tree and up into the hill. It was a room which besides being cosy, somehow managed to be part of the garden.

I had inherited from my father's father a Pye Black Box, which dated from the early fifties. It was made of solid, heavy wood and was the forerunner to hi-fi, having the innovation of two speakers - one at port and one at starboard. It had a remarkably mellow tone and enhanced kitchen activities with its music. My grandfather had loved music, my grandmother had not. A Forsytian character, parsimonious with money, he eventually treated himself to this extravagance for his study, where he could listen and enjoy in peace. He died in 1957, so he can have wallowed a mere four or five years in his collection of records which included Beethoven symphonies, Chopin's restful nocturnes, a number of Gilbert and Sullivan operas, and enough Rossini to convince me that I preferred his 'Cenerentola' to his 'Barbiere'. These records came to me along with the venerable machine, and of course we added many LPs of our own.

Nelle would sit on top of the throb of music, her feet tucked under her bosom as she absorbed the Brahm's 'Double Concerto', the whole of Tchaikovsky's 'Eugene Onegin', several albums of Ralph McTell's songs and Dave Swarbrick's fiddle 'tossing the feathers' with Fairport Convention. Marion who lived next door, reckoned she could tell my mood by opening her own back door and tasting the musical flavour of the day pouring from our kitchen. Nelle liked all music equally: opera, folk, pop, piano, so long as she could sit on me, on the music machine or any other surface where she felt part of the proceedings, she did not mind, her pink nose twitching, she enjoyed it all.

Haiku (on stealing)

Cats never steal, they
merely take what they feel they
are entitled to.

Chapter Eighteen

Jenkins' Jungle, The Roof, and Harris

The proceedings in the kitchen left little opportunity for gardening. I persevered as best I could, but was becoming discouraged. Graham had less and less time as his job became more demanding, and there was a great deal I could not tackle because it was too heavy. Until these jobs were done, my more creative ideas were useless. We felt the garden was beginning to run away from us and we cast around for help, using the network of contacts we had built in Macclesfield.

Dodo, as she was affectionately known, had babysat for Mike and Marion next door for years, and had helped us out when our young-and-fun team of sitters went unavailable. We were all fond of her and knew her to be as reliable as the turn of seasons. Accordingly, I asked Dodo if she could recommend someone to help us in the garden. Typically obliging, but cautious, she said she thought she might do, but that it could take a little while to find the right person. Respecting Dodo's judgement, along with her ability to age gracefully in make-up, pearls, spaniel-brown eyes and young heart, we were content to wait. Sure enough, a few weeks later, Graham and the garden were viewed by Mr Jenkins - in his early seventies, blue-eyed, straight backed, a veteran of Egypt in the Second World War, he pronounced, "It's a bit of a jungle, but I think I can do something with it." Graham told him that we were thinking of three or four hours per week but that I was the boss he needed to talk to. They arranged for him to call again the next afternoon to see me, the financial arrangements being a pound an hour. This was less than half the going rate, but Mr Jenkins was as rigid as his shoulders and the price could not be talked up no matter how we pleaded.

Nor could he be persuaded to call me by my first name, which would have been so much easier, as he found "Melmoth" an impossible mouthful and always addressed me as "Mrs Mmmm..ermum."

Mr Jenkins announced himself as "an earth and stones man." This meant that he was meticulous in removing stones from the soil and was tireless in his attempts to improve it, to make it friable and rich from compost. He was so thorough that I would have backed him to find the smallest needle in the largest haystack. It would take him three or four hours to weed a small area that I could have made tidy to my satisfaction in half an hour. But my idea of tidy was not his. When he'd weeded an area it was cowed into staying that way for a long time.

The same could not be said of the stones, who were a determined brigade. The afternoon air would be punctuated by Mr Jenkins' distinctive light cough and the clink of stones into his bucket as he gathered them, then used them to help fill the potholes in the lane, but no matter how many bucketfuls he removed there were always more to come. Between ourselves we began to wonder if stones can breed, or seed themselves or even fly, for they soon disappeared again from the potholes, probably returning to the soft earth where they felt more comfortable.

Mr Jenkins and I had a healthy respect for one another. He knew how to tame the garden by working methodically through each rough area. He specialised in growing vegetables, as we discovered once he had reduced the jungle to something he considered manageable. "Water with the spade," he would say as he dug deep trenches, and "Keep your plants aired," as he hoed round the growth he had encouraged, emulating the farmers of North Africa. At first he had plans to enlarge the vegetable garden by incorporating into it the area I had always kept for compost and garden rubbish. However, he conceded that we needed to keep this as a utility area when he saw the piles of hedge clippings and old shrubs climb to a mountain as he proceeded with jungle clearance.

****

There were moments when we clashed, for our respective ideas on how gardens should look were often at opposite ends of the lawn. Mr Jenkins wanted plants neat, tidy at the edges, pruned to precision, staked to attention. I think plants should flow, spill over onto paths, fulfil their natural shape......

There was an early flowering rhododendron, whose crinoline form fell gracefully onto the corner of the front lawn, giving me pleasure all the year round, the pink flowers being a party frock worn for a short time, a bonus, but not essential to my enjoyment of the plant, as seen constantly from the kitchen window. It was a beautiful shape.

I came home one afternoon to find Mr Jenkins trimming the rhododendron's hemline well clear of its ankles, and to my horrified, *"OH, MR JENKINS!!!"* he had an irrefutable reply:

"But Mrs Mmmm..ermum, you can't get to the soil underneath with all those leaves in the way low down."

84

Why anyone should *want* to get to the soil underneath was beyond me, what I did know was that my view from the kitchen window had become a sorrow instead of a pleasure. I grieved for that lost hemline. The rhododendron was now just a bush, and although I vetoed any further attacks on its person, it has never recovered the full floating charm of its glossy skirt.

Mr Jenkins was also a believer in mortar. Ideally he thought it should smooth over as much rough stone as possible. One day when he was stabilising the stone wall that is the border between the lane and front garden (just beyond the ankle length rhododendron) I hinted in vain that we did actually rather like seeing the stone, and that we did not want the wall to have the appearance of almond paste awaiting royal icing.

"Oh, but Mrs Mmmm..ermum, you need plenty of mortar, otherwise it won't stay firm."

Miraculously, Graham had come home early that day, and was sent out by his helpless general to deploy tanks to repel the mortar attack. This took tact, courage and more tact, but the battle was more or less won, for the wall today is recognisable as a stone wall not a cake, despite some remaining traces of over enthusiastic marzipan.

****

Mr Jenkins and I had our differing views, but we valued his kindly nature and his tireless work on our behalf. He would think nothing of arriving at twelve and working through till six in the evening. We were often paying him £14 or £15 per week for his devoted hours. He was not slow, but he was sure and thorough. We could not have hoped for better value for our £1 per hour! Slowly the garden came round to looking well tended, and Mr Jenkins and I came to a mutual understanding and respect for each other's stances. As he grew older he spent more and more time with his beloved vegetables and fruit. If you costed them in terms of Mr Jenkins' time and effort and the money we paid him, even at £1 an hour they must have been among the most expensive organically grown vegetables in the country. Moreover, the rabbits inevitably ate the lettuces, and with all the care lavished on the strawberrries, the avid weeding, the underlaying with straw and overcovering with netting, we were lucky to achieve a trio of fruit that were worth eating. This was a puzzle until one day I surprised a squirrel having a merry time with the best of the fruit. I discovered as he wriggled through and scampered away, a neat hole in the netting where he had been organising his secret one rodent raiding party. It nearly drove me to dispatch the strawberry plants, but that would have upset Mr Jenkins, so they stayed for him to minister unto and for the squirrel to enjoy.

It was only after Mr Jenkins had retired from battle and the strawberries got minimal attention that they responded the next season by yielding a glorious crop, and they have done so every year since. There are still squirrels, but no netting is no challenge, and if there is no challenge perhaps the fruit no longer tastes as sweet. Whatever the reason, the squirrel has ceded us the strawberry crop, and we are grateful.

With Mr Jenkins' help, spaces were created in the front garden so that I could try to achieve some colour all the year round. It was a painful decision to remove four out of ten of the winter flowering cherries, but they were choking and stifling each other's growth.

I am as capable as the next person of critically muttering about people who have planted trees and shrubs too close together. "Why ever did they do it?" I have said many times and then proceeded to make the same mistakes myself, for it is somehow impossible to visualise a tree at its mature spread as you tenderly tread the earth round the spindly stick of a so-called sapling. Moreover, what if you have only planted the one and that dies on you? Years of growing time could be wasted, whereas if you put in two or three where one should do, you have some spares. I suppose that is the theory, but then if they all flourish, you have to find good homes for the spares, lifting them before they grow too big, risking murdering them in the process. It is a conundrum which few of us ever solve satisfactorily, and it only serves to enhance admiration for Capability Brown, whom we think of as having planted trees exactly where they would, eventually, look perfect, waiting with confidence and patience for them to grow, apparently not minding in the least that he would not live long enough to see the full beauty of his landscapes fulfilled. It is a comfort to know that it was not quite like that; for some of his plantings at least, he transported virtually mature trees from special nurseries, a technique previously used to create the gardens at Versailles for Louis XIV.

Fortunately for me, the front garden did not require any more trees. I concentrated on shrubs that would flower when the blues of May had faded, hypericums, the good-tempered potentillas, and hydrangeas. One of Mr Jenkins' triumphs had been to encourage from quiet misery to glowing glory a blue hydrangea that was huddled against the nasty holly when we arrived. In recent years, its depth of colour in the late summer is a lasting tribute to his skills. I have been almost as pleased with my own effort in planting *Hydrangea sargentiana*, which is a large variety with leaves of velvet friendliness and lacecap flowers, as wide as they are beautiful. This impressive plant's essential

claim to fame is its enjoyment of deep shade, so that it flourishes in two difficult, dark places of the garden, brightening them with white doyleys for weeks
of the late summer, and causing comment from visitors and passers-by.

****

There was landscaping of a kind to do on the house. Old houses are always in
need of some face-lift or other, and we had had damp in a chimney breast
which had been competently sorted by a small-scale builder. We then asked
him if he could undertake some roof repairs for us and he readily agreed. Work
began. After three weeks the spare room was ankle deep in rubble, the rafters
open to polythene and sky and we were about to depart on holiday for two
weeks. This could have been a sensible move, as most of the house tasted of
dust. However, we fondly hoped that work would be completed while we
were away, and when Tom said that he could not actually progress without
more money up front, I thought this seemed reasonable. I therefore gave him
a cheque for £500. A gross error. I now know to my cost that you *never* pay in
advance. In my naive way I had assumed everyone must feel as I do, that if
someone pays you in advance you are beholden to deliver yesterday, if not
sooner. But there is another ethic which apparently says, "Why bother to do the
work if you've got the money in your pocket already?"

We came back from holiday to find the situation had not moved forward an
iota, except that the rubble level seemed to have risen. A phone call to Tom
elicited the reasonable and logical response that there was a wasps' nest on one
of the beams, so he could not proceed until it had been removed.

We had it removed. We informed him that we had had it removed. He did not
come. We phoned. Tom was busy on other jobs. He did not come. We phoned.
He would come tomorrow. He did not come.....

This went on for weeks until the good weather broke. It began to rain. Water
began to seep into the house. Water began to drip down the walls, through the
ceiling, ruining the surface of the dining room table.

We wrote a 'Bye bye Tom letter', wrote off the £500 to my stupidity, and for the
first time ever, Graham pulled strings at work. Two days later the house felt like
a state of emergency, with men on the roof and up the walls, the smell of pitch,
the flap of felt, the heave of slate and the flame of oxy-acetylene. The roof was
mended, the gully between the two roofs releaded, the rubble skipped away.
In the silence rose Ron with his healing white paint and rolls of wallpaper.
Soon, blessedly soon, in time for Graham's mum to come to stay, the house

would be again as we had almost forgotten it.

****

In the midst of the restoring therapy was Harris.

She had appeared on my parents' doorstep in search of a quieter home than the one shared with nine or ten other cats and their continual offspring. She felt that her middle age deserved peace, and worked on my parents until they gave in to her demands. She was a strange squat shape, brindled, and with a question mark for a tail where it had once been broken. My parents' sweet natured collie-mix dog, was unsure of this intrusion into her home and tried actively to discourage visits. This prompted my father to say, "Cindy, don't harass the cat."

Once Harris had a name it was not long before her patience was rewarded. She moved in and gave birth to three kittens, one of whom, Tigger, they kept till he was tragically run over. My mother and father grieved for him more than his mother did. She settled back to being lady of all she surveyed, though made gracious allowances for Cindy's longstanding ownership of my parents.

****

The Year of the Roof at Throstles' Nest was also the year my parents decided to move from West Mersea in Essex, to be near us in Macclesfield. Everyone thought it best for it to happen before Christmas, as the weather has a habit of turning nasty in early January. They were to move out on 17th December and to arrive up here on the 18th. My parents were rightly concerned as to how best to see Harris through the move, and felt it best if she travelled ahead.

As it happened, Graham and I had to be at a posh 'do' in London in early December, so I arranged to travel down to Essex the morning after it, collect Harris from my mother at Colchester station, then return, cat in basket, via London back to Macclesfield.

The weather had turned Siberian cold during my inter-city journey from Cheshire to London, and after the 'do' I remember skating round the outside of St Paul's in a full length evening frock on high heels. The pavements formed a continuous ice rink. There were no taxis to be hailed, either because they had already been taken by perished fares, or because they were hibernating till morning.

My inter-city ticket had been booked with Graham's as a business journey, so

Harris and I travelled back from Euston first class, which she deemed fitting. We got to know each other well on that journey, which she seemed to enjoy, taking the train and other people very much in her stride. I was able to have the lid of the basket open so that we could communicate properly.

Under normal circumstances she would have come home with me and taken up residence in the spare bedroom, where she would have felt part of the household without the danger of upsets with Moses, Aaron or Nelle. Unfortunately, circumstances were far from normal, for at this point in the month the spare room was still resonant with departed rubble, our bedroom piled with extra furniture, and the house generally in mountainous disarray. The disarray was scheduled to be swiftly demolished, but this would be immediately replaced by a resident in the spare room, my mum-in-law.

I had played down all these inconveniences to my parents, as I felt they had enough to concern them in the upheaval of their move, but I had to confess that the only sensible and safe course for Harris would be for her to go into a highly acclaimed cattery until their arrival.

As we arrived at Macclesfield station on 8th December the first snow was falling. I drove with Harris the two miles up into the hills, and left her apparently unconcerned, in her comfortable chamber with heater and kindly care. Nonetheless, I felt a traitor and hated leaving her.

The next two or three days were spent setting the house to rights in preparation for Graham's mum's arrival on the Sunday. She lived in Broadstairs with Graham's brother, wife and family, but we had her to stay with us every six months or so. This year they had booked a winter holiday in Florida so we had promised to have mum for longer than usual, and she would be with us till well after Christmas.

Graham set off on the Sunday to drive to Scratchwood services at the bottom of the M1. This was the meeting point for mum's journeys. During the afternoon the snow began again in earnest so that Graham worried as he fought his way through the swirling whiteness if he was going to get home safely with his elderly passenger, or whether they would be trapped in a snowdrift. Mum, still an optimist, and with an innocent faith in her younger son, was quite unconcerned about possible danger. This faith paid off for they arrived safely, the blizzard pelting the air with its feathers which by morning had filled the drive. We were snowed in.

It was a day when no one tried too hard to get to work or to school. It was

Snow Monday and we enjoyed it. However, if my poor parents had had all known weather patterns for a British winter fed into several computers, they could not have chosen more difficult icy weather in which to move house. We have lived in Cheshire for nearly twenty years, experiencing mainly mild winters. Certainly, 1981 has been the only one in which winter clamped down with such determined ferocity so early.

The previous owners of my parents' new home had moved out on 17th December, so I was able to skid round that evening and do some preparing of the way, installing a Christmas tree ablaze with lights.

The journey up from Essex, though icy, was successfully accomplished, and Dorothy and I had the house more or less straight by the time the travellers arrived in the late afternoon. The best part though, came the next day, winding my way between the banked drifts of snow on narrow lanes, up to the cattery to collect Harris. She had eaten well, and appeared contented enough, being a cat with incurable optimism about human beings. However, her rapture on seeing me was then outshone by her radiant purrings on rediscovering my parents. She did not mind at all that the house was different. She was home, with them, for Christmas.

Chapter Nineteen

"...more things in heaven and earth..."

The next twelve months were spent giving time to my parents, helping them to settle into their new surroundings. My father had been reluctant to move, and with his usual enjoyed pessimism had announced, "This move is going to kill me. I'll be dead before I arrive, you'll see." My mother had been determined to come, feeling the need for more family support in caring for my father. However, once up here, she found it more difficult than he did. She thought the town ugly, she missed the sea and the wide skies of East Anglia. He, on the other hand, had his armchair same as usual, and once the weather eventually turned warmer could take his slow-slow walk round the block with Cindy, striking up new acquaintances as he went. He was good at chatting to people and soon had quite a social round. Moreover, Graham would visit every Saturday and they would enjoy watching cricket or rugger together. Graham got on very well with my father for whom this was the high spot of the week.

Fortunately, we had no crystal ball to spoil our enjoyment of their first Christmas up here. It was good to be all together, and the two mums, who had been good friends for years, were delighted to be able to spend plenty of time *tête à tête*, while Harris purred her satisfaction at reunion with home.

It was not far into the New Year, however, that it became clear that she was ill. Her little squat body was found to be full of cancer and there was nothing to be done. Harris had had a hard time for most of her life but was pampered at the end and that is the memory to keep. I missed her funny cross face nearly as much as my parents did, and after an interval of two or three months, knowing that my mother was still feeling the gap, said to her, "Mother you need a cat."

My father's reaction was predictable, "We don't want another cat, it would only be a worry at our age."

My mother and I did not take too much notice, and at last a ginger tom kitten was tracked down, exactly as she had requested. We drove to the far side of Manchester to collect Barnaby, who was white with splodges of marmalade. He took an instant shine to my mum.

We had prepared the way by telling my father that we were "just going to look", so he pretended enraged surprise when we arrived back with our small bundle....

"I thought I said we didn't want a cat!"

Cats have a way with them though. Within a week my father's voice could be heard from the depth of his chair plaintively calling, "Where's my pussycat then?"

Barnaby was a winner and grew to be heavyweight with it.

****

It was one day that summer which produced the most treasured memory of Timma. She was an ideal dog for a writer to take for a walk, as she left you to your thoughts and mutterings while she explored and followed likely rabbit trails, always appearing later when you needed her.

The hill and sky were the classic green and blue of summer which was a rare treat in a year mainly distinguished by greyness. We had walked to the top of the hill to taste the horizon which then rolled away towards Buxton. I was absorbed in my thoughts as I made my way back down the hill, across the track and came down the field to the gate that led back into the garden. Then I remembered Timma and turned to call her. There she was, deer-dainty, dark against the blue of sky, pursuing a scent. She was about half a mile away. I cupped my hands and called long and loud and shrill. The sound froze her to the skyline as she registered my voice, then she responded with the speed, grace and loyalty for which we loved her. She came because she wanted to, she came as fast as she could down the steepest part of the hill, disappearing for a moment into a fold, then downward and onward till she crossed the track and took the field. She arrived laughing, scarcely puffed, enjoying my pleasure at her display. She was fit and life was fun. I thought back to that moment, when embroiled in the weird year that was about to come.

****

The first two months of 1983 passed uneventfully until we redecorated what we called the 'family' or 'flop' room. It was a thorough redecoration, including a new carpet and a new television. After a few days of congratulating ourselves on how good it looked, we had our abortive burglars.

They were very unlucky, as Graham was at his miracles again. He had taken a day's holiday that Monday, come home from the town about an hour ahead of me, noticed the front door open, a strange car in the courtyard opposite, had a vague feeling of unease, and had the presence of mind to leave his car blocking the lane. He met the two burglars in the narrow passage by the kitchen. They were carrying the new television, a tape recorder and a cassette holder full of tapes. Graham had the advantage of surprise and they obeyed his command to "Put that lot down, *carefully,* and get out!" Having got out, they could not retrieve their car on which finger prints matched those in the house. They were soon apprehended. We had been lucky and thought little more about it.

Then in April, work began to replace the wooden shack masquerading as a garage for a proper one, built in Cheshire brick, with a slate roof; solid as the house of the third little pig. Cheshire brick is a recycled commodity. The bricks are taken from old buildings that have been demolished, often they have traces of paint still on them, and they have the mellowness of age.

Mr Jenkins voiced his disapproval: "Oh, Mrs Mmm...ermum, I can't think why you want to go spending all that money building a nice garage like that using half worn out bricks...not wise at all."

By then our folly was far advanced. On the first day of the project, the builders had delivered their "young lad" to demolish the shack and he probably had the easiest day of his apprenticeship as the whole thing collapsed inside ten minutes. I think he just leant on it with one finger and gave a gentle shove. The resulting space was already an improvement.

The Blue Peter balcony condemned as "unsafe" by the surveyor in charge of building the garage, dropped off the wall in a quick flick of the wrist, and we blanched to remember Graham's mum sitting up there enjoying the view on many an occasion, unaware that the drawing pins could have popped and the double-sided sticky tape snapped at any moment. In its place was to be a solid construction built on steel girders sunk several feet into the ground and then disguised as pillars of brick - half worn out, of course. The balustrade would be of wood with properly turned uprights as used on internal stairs, the balcony becoming a venue worthy of any Juliet instead of a tacky eyesore.

****

There was much digging and clearing away of soil during April and May, for to create the new garage we needed to cut back a long way into the garden. You can of course argue, that what followed in that strange year, was an unrelated sequence of incidents linked only by flukes of chance. But I have found myself asking whether there could have been an underlying reason; a negative force, some kind of psychic energy disturbance stimulated by the work we were doing. Whatever the cause - or lack of it - the cumulative effect of ensuing events came to feel peculiarly sinister.

****

Early in June, on the first hot day of what was to be a good summer, a boy of seventeen was drowned in the top reservoir. We received the knock on the door, the panicked teenage girl, made the phone calls and offered what comfort we could.

A week later, on a Sunday afternoon, a young woman standing peacefully by Swan's Pool feeding the ducks with her two year old daughter in a pushchair, was hit by a drunken driver. We came on the scene just after the accident had happened and I went with mother and child in the ambulance to the hospital.

Three days later was the day that Nelle went to have some teeth out. It was a hot day in a hot summer, the kind of weather where cats stay out at night, stroll in for ad hoc meals, make love to the catmint and perform ecstatic floor exercises, polishing the hard warmth of the crazy paving with their elastic limbed fur. Nelle was good at this, her pale pink carnation of a nose beaming contentment from her white face with its black smudges. But this particular morning her nose was no more pleased than her disappointed yellow eyes, which alighted on no breakfast. No breakfast for her, while behind the study door Moses and Aaron tucked into their normal platefuls, plus milk. Did she remember that as a small grubby stray, on her arrival five years ago, it was she who had benefited from delicious food in the study, while the older, bigger cats curiously absorbed her presence under the door? Nelle was affronted, even though the pain in her mouth (which caused her to drool deceptively) kept hunger low level. It was the principle.

However, she trusted the hands that lifted her gently into the wicker basket, which she rather liked, and resigned herself to the car ride. Nelle made the most of life, and when left at the vet's on this morning, she was not alarmed; not pleased, but sensing that everything was well intended.

After I had delivered Nelle to the vet, I was going shopping, as we had friends coming for a meal. They had been having a difficult time for one reason or another and we had thought we would try to cheer them up. I also planned to visit the victims of Sunday's accident. Suddenly I remembered that I had left Moses and Aaron shut in the study, so I rushed home to let them out, with profuse apologies, before going to shop and then to make my hospital visit. If only I had forgotten them.

****

I had been home less than five minutes, laden as only a packhorse or a woman can be, when Hazel appeared:

"Jenny, something very sad has happened."

She had returned home earlier in the day to find one of my cats lying stiff on her doorstep, his head so badly smashed in that it was nearly impossible to tell which one it was. It must have been a horrible shock for her. She had wrapped him very beautifully and I found him lying in the garden shed. I suppose I knew it was Aaron, but could not bear to think of his innocent trust having been so brutally shattered. I delayed that knowledge, almost too shocked to cry, feeling that it would be marginally easier to bear if it were Moses - at least he roamed further. It made more sense, but deep down as well, was the knowledge and guilt, that I loved Aaron more, had felt closer to him.

Mr Jenkins was gardening and I asked him to dig a grave in one of Moses' favourite places. An hour later however, as I was toying with unpacking the shopping, I heard a deep sad yowl from the open back door. I knew that sound could only have come from Moses, and rushed to pick him up, trying to stamp down my confused and guilty feelings that I would rather have been holding Aaron.

I asked Mr Jenkins to dig another grave, this time in the spot where Aaron had so often dozed, under the laburnum tree among the snow-in-summer.

I rang Graham's secretary to ask her to warn him of what had happened. He remembers her being puzzled at my obvious distress — it was only a cat, after all. At that time she had never owned a cat herself, but in later years she was to have four, and to become an even more devoted cat person than me.

Next I rang the vet, my hand shaking as I dialled the number, for whenever a general anaesthetic is involved there is always a slight risk of the patient not coming through. Nelle, however, was fine, her pleasure at being home again, a ray of sun on a bleak day.

Somehow I got a meal together, and we struggled through the evening, but only because I had asked Hazel to ring our guests to explain what had happened, telling them not to say anything, but to understand if we were somewhat subdued.

****

The next day was a busy one, my mother was away for a few days, and I was keeping an eye on my father, going in to make his breakfast, and sometimes his lunch or his tea as well. I could not yet bring myself to talk about what had happened, at least not without danger of soggy breakdown. In the end I delayed the news till my mother's return at the weekend.

Meanwhile, because the day was mapped out that Thursday, I carried on as normally as I could. There were few private moments to grieve. I staggered through The Darby and Joan Club, where I have helped for years, by saying I thought I might have a cold coming. Together, Graham and I went to the German evening class, though I would have much rather have stayed at home. However, it was the last lesson of the year and we had all taken a little exam the previous week which we knew the teacher would want to discuss. I pushed myself to go, and paid the price, as I only embarrassed everyone, including myself, by collapsing into tears near the end of the two hours, in response to an innocuous question about giving directions in German. And that was the end of German for Beginners Year One. The students melted away rather quietly.

People grieve in different ways and heal at different speeds. I know now that I need time to myself to do it deeply but privately, or shared non-verbally with only the closest of companions. Only after that stage is it helpful to talk about it. It is also exhausting, so space needs to be made to allow for that, and whether a pet or a parent the pain can be intense.

Where there is anticipatory grieving, as when you know someone has a terminal illness, you are able to prepare yourself for what is to come, take comfort from small remissions and from precious time spent with the person you are going to lose. When it happens, it hurts and you continue to grieve, but the actual loss is a part of the process that has been borne for a while. When the bereavement is brutally sudden you are entering the process at the very beginning, plunged into icy waters with no warning, you are in a state of shock, and shock can kill people, certainly make them ill. It should never be underestimated nor taken lightly.

It also helps if there are no further disasters.

****

The week after Aaron was killed, Rudolf Nureyev was dancing at the Palace Theatre in Manchester. He had decreed that some tickets should be kept in reserve to be sold on the day of the performance. By the Wednesday it seemed time to try to cheer up. I left home with Graham at seven in the morning arriving near eight to join the massive queue consisting of one other keenie and me. Obtaining tickets was not, therefore, a problem and I was home by half past ten. The plan was to catch a train into Manchester again about six o'clock that evening.

Nelle had not appeared that morning when I gave Moses his breakfast, but it had been very early and I had assumed that she was still busy on the night shift. By five o'clock when there was still no sign of her in response to regular calling through the afternoon, I was getting extremely anxious. At last, I found her, tucked deep into the airing cupboard. I could see there was something badly wrong. I lifted her out and took her out into the garden for some air. She was shaky on her legs, but began to move around slowly. I watched mesmerised as she made her way unsteadily from the paved area near the back door till she reached the wrought iron gate in the wall, where she loved to sunbask. She went through the gate, along the path, up the two steps onto the lawn, staggered the short distance onto the flowerbed, and there, under the laburnum tree, she heaved her heart up on Aaron's grave.

Afterwards, the vet dismissed the idea that Aaron's death could have made Nelle ill, saying she had had a very nasty virus, but it seemed too much of a coincidence. And why in a garden of our size should she choose that place to go to vomit?

I was all for cancelling Rudolf Nureyev, but fortunately our young baby-sitter had a car, arrived early and was very firm. She insisted that we must go. She would take Nelle to the vet. It was as well she did, for when I rang from the theatre to check, the news was that she had indeed been very poorly and we could have lost her. As it was, the patient responded quickly to the course of antibiotics and made a full recovery. But we were right to wonder "What next?" for the year still had plenty of unpleasant tricks to play.

****

Nelle was scarcely well when there was another death in the neighbourhood. This time it was Sue, the farmer's daughter who used to deliver our milk to us in our early years at Throstles' Nest. She was a keen horsewoman and we had been used to seeing her working with the horses in the field behind the house. All too soon after her marriage and the birth of her daughter, she became mysteriously ill with what later proved to be Motor Neurone Disease. This appalling illness can move with lethal speed, and in an effort to slow it, an experimental treatment was sometimes offered. It consisted of the patient lying in something resembling a diver's bell with a similar decompressing effect. Sue, who could

97

not even lift a flannel to cool her face, found the experience terrifying and would only agree to go into this tomb-like contraption if accompanied. I had been with her on three occasions, for though I had found it far from pleasant I had managed to keep her reasonably relaxed, so that after the first time she asked for me again. I was glad to go for Sue's sake, and inevitably in those confined conditions grew close to her. She was someone I had hardly known before these sessions, but I felt I'd lost a friend when she died.

****

The hooter packed up on my car. A minor blip, though my father with his usual festive air commented, "Well Mary, (his pet name for me) you ought to get that fixed. You never know when a lorry might be backing into you, and you'll need to hoot to warn it off. What would you do then?"

"Oh father, *really!*" I laughed.

Three days later I was in a car park in my pale blue mini, when a large furniture van with those nastily sharp corners on its backside reversed towards me. The film turned slowly, I heard my father's voice, saw the lack of escape space and wondered whether the driver would hear me if I shouted. One of the murderous corners made contact with my door, fortunately as it did so, the driver realised the situation and stopped, but it made a dent in the door, and a quake in my narrowly avoided chest. It was almost worth it though to see my father's face on being told how right he had been, and how close we had come to a thundering good disaster.

The next weekend Graham nearly severed a finger on the lawn mower. The finger went septic, and he became suddenly allergic to penicillin causing his feet to puff like éclairs. We needed a break.

****

On the way to our Welsh holiday the car had an argument with a wall on a narrow bridge, and in separating the two combatants Graham lost the gold signet ring I had given him. However, we can't count that as a proper disaster for on the way home we had a good hunt by daylight and the owner reclaimed his treasure from the rock. This could have been an encouraging sign that life was about to return to a more normal balanced sequence of ups and downs. Not so. I began to feel as if I were taking part in a continuous boxing match in which there was not even the fair play of breaks between rounds. No convenient bell rang as I tottered to my feet, before life took another swipe at us.

Come the autumn, both our sons were struggling to settle into new schools and this produced all kinds of traumas as any parent knows, including Hugo running away from school, or home, or was it both? He had not run very far — just up the field. However, we were not to know this and we felt we should inform the police as well as his headteacher. A jolly morning was enjoyed by all!

While all this was going on, my mum-in-law had come to stay for her usual two weeks and at this stage in her life she needed a lot of time, love and care devoted to her. This was hardly her fault, but it may have been what finally sucked me dry. I developed a horrendous cold that virtually stopped me breathing, a septic finger from a splinter, and thrush as a side effect from the antibiotics. My colour by now was that of pale green pastry and I had as much energy as a squashed banana.

The doctor took a peak inside my eyes and promptly sent me for a blood test, which revealed a haemoglobin count so low as to make me a candidate for instant transfusion. I chose the path of heavy iron tablets and began to feel a little better. It may be that I had neglected myself to some extent under my newly fumbling vegetarian diet, but I thought it had more to do with the events of the year. It was as if I had been bleeding internally for several months. No wonder the blood count was so low.

This analogy hit me with force when soon after the incident with the lorry in the car park, I cracked open an egg and the inside was a flood of blood. I have never seen an egg like it, before or since. As an isolated incident I might have thought little about it, but among the other happenings of that summer I was vulnerable and felt threatened. Home had always been a haven, the vicinity in which we lived so safe. Now I felt there was menace in the air. It was unnerving.

****

The building work was completed by early autumn, my body responded swiftly to the iron, and the disaster rate slowed down. However, in November the poetry group of which I had been a longstanding member began to disintegrate taking some valued friendships with it, and in December Hazel and her family moved to a house in the country on the other side of the town. It was only a few miles away, and I had known the move was coming, of course, but I also knew I would miss her terribly, for it could not be the same as being able to pop in on one another, as we had always done. The boxer was on the canvas yet again.

****

Through all these events there was always the problem of Moses and his insatiable grief for his lost friend. It was a hot summer and he spent most of it either sitting on Aaron's grave, or yowling pitifully. It was heart-rending and there seemed little we could do to comfort him. This was another reason why it was harder for Moses to be the one left behind. He was not a naturally cuddly cat. Aaron and I would have comforted each other. Moses and I did not have that close bond. I tried. He tried. One day when I was upstairs I heard him crying under the laburnum tree, went down, picked him up and sat with him on my lap for an hour or so. On that occasion he did allow me to comfort him, but it was hit and miss and his grief did not seem to ease with time. He and Nelle grew marginally closer together, but what he needed was a substitute Aaron.

In September I felt we could start making enquiries about Colourpoint kittens. For Moses' sake it seemed imperative to find a kitten of the same breed in the hope that he would take to it. But my phone calls proved fruitless. No one had any Colourpoint kittens. There seemed no sense in seeking any other kind of cat, so I eventually gave up, thinking we would try again in the spring, when the breeders would have plenty of available kittens.

Moses continued to be miserable, we continued to have problems. It felt like a good idea for this year to come to an end; the quicker the better. The new year had to be kinder, surely.

Six days before Christmas, a few days after Hazel had moved, I was driving round to my parents about five o'clock. It was dark of course. As I drove along a familiar road bordered by a park on one side, I saw a shape lying in the road. Two or three oncoming cars passed over it, not touching it, but sooner or later the shape would be reduced to a flat silhouette against the tarmac.

I effected a U-turn as fast as I could, planted my car protectively in front of the body, and went to investigate. The shape was not a dead one - it was unconscious but breathing with a rasping rattle which sounded far from healthy. I picked it up, limp and warm, keeping it on my lap as I pulled the car to the side of the road, then knocked on the nearest door.

I was lucky. A pleasant woman answered who registered instant concern. Together we rang the vet and arranged for me to take the patient straight to the surgery.

The assessment was that this crumpled heap of black and white would survive, though he had a fractured jaw, a damaged pelvis and as the vet said, "a very bad headache." He would need to remain in veterinary care for a week or two.

He was reckoned to be six months old, which meant that he could have been born the very day that Aaron died. I like to think that he was.

That evening, Graham, the boys and I talked it over, and we all felt that a decision had been taken for us. We would pay for the hospitalisation of this squashed moggy and then give him a home in the hope that Moses would like him. Somehow I felt that he would, that the fates were at last on our side.

I rang every two or three days to check progress and on 30th December was told, "You can take your cat home tomorrow."

We were all excited, and for once naming the new arrival presented no difficulty. We were still studying German with the same patient teacher, the day of collection was 31st December, the German for New Year's Eve is *'Silvester'*. Our sons identified the name with the cartoon cat, so they approved the choice, but for us it represented far more. It was a farewell to the bad old year and a greeting to a new and happier one. Silvester would be a symbol and a hope.

We were expecting a lot of him.

Chapter Twenty

Silvester

Graham came with me to collect Silvester and I could see his face fall as our much vaunted angel of hope was brought into the surgery and lifted onto the table by the vet. The animal's long coat was drab, as dull and lifeless as a well used blackboard, while his intended white trims were reminiscent of Nelle rising from the boiler. He was scrawny as a lopsided caterpillar, with a crooked mouth, a peg tooth and a pronounced limp.

"Well now," said the vet cheerfully, "He's a great little chap isn't he? He's going to be a lovely cat."

The enthusiasm was infectious, after all the vet was much better acquainted with Silvester than we were. It was explained that his jaw was still wired up but could be released in a week's time. The limp would lessen with time and his coat and personality would flourish in a good home.

We paid the fifty pound bill and took our important new family member home in the cat basket, where he did not protest at all. He was installed in the guest room which would be his base for the next few days, while he grew accustomed to us, the house, its sounds and scents and other occupants.

As I lifted Silvester from the basket and began stroking him he showed no sign of alarm, emitting not one, but several chirrups of pleasure.

It was an unusual New Year's Eve, as I spent hours of it lying on the spare room bed reading, with a convalescent cat on my chest. Silvester was very physical and soon made it clear that he was one for a cuddle. This quiet time we spent together allowed us to start to know one another. Bonding was begun. Late in the evening I took him down to the drawing room to introduce him to the coal fire and to meet Graham again. Our new number three cat walked all round the room, not stealthily but with confidence, the only hesitations caused by his limping gait, which was very pronounced.

The boys' initial response to Silvester was more outspokenly honest than ours had been. They pronounced him "dead scruffy." They had a point, but only one, scruffy he certainly was, dead - he was not. Gradually the life in him strengthened. He was still very young and had suffered severe trauma; knocked from a pleasant adventure in the park into unconsciousness, pain, bright lights and a stranger sticking wires in his mouth. It could have been enough to give a cat personality problems.

Instead, Silvester responded to us all with affection and good humour in his rapidly healing body. Whatever his past history might have been he did not hold it against us. I groomed him gently to try to improve his coat while he was unable to tend it himself, but once the wire was removed from his jaw and he could eat more comfortably he also began to wash himself as thoroughly as any other cat. His slush-toned paws became snow shoes and were as big. He has enormous feet, so much so that one of his nicknames is 'Bigfoot'. When he is pounding on you, you are very much aware of having a cat in your lap, particularly as in his ecstasy the claws come out. It is thought that 'pounding' is a leftover habit from kittenhood, when it encouraged the mother's milk to flow more freely. This being so, Silvester would not win prizes in anatomy, as he is not averse to giving me cranial massage when I am trying to sleep! The hugeness of his feet is only outsized by the dimensions of his whiskers, which seemed to grow inches in weeks as he matured, till they would not disgrace the demeanour of a full grown leopard, and give a new meaning to the term extrasensory perception.

Soon after Silvester arrived, a gripping serial began on television. It was shown in the original German with subtitles, and much of Britain identified with the decent men in the submarine *'Das Boot'*, especially with the sensistive captain. We held our breath with the crew as the ASDIC (underwater radar) of the British destroyer sought them out "..blip..blip..blip..blip..blip.." threatening to discover them and to depth-charge them out of existence.

You could hear Silvester approaching in the same way, "chrrp..chrrp..chrrp..chrrp..chrrp.." Had we been struggling for a name, Asdic would have done nicely, except that there was nothing destructive about this radar operator. As Graham remarked, "If he were a bloke, everyone would say, 'What a thoroughly nice chap.'" The constant chirruping was his way of circumventing his rusted up purr. It did not work any more. Maybe it had seized up with the shock of the accident, but for a cat of his cheerful disposition it must have been frustrating, and it was strange to handle a blatantly happy cat with no purr.

****

Meanwhile there had been introductions to make. Both Nelle and Moses had been sniffing under the spareroom door during the first week of Silvester's arrival. They were curious to meet him. However, we thought it best to leave the big moment until Silvester was a little more convalescent, acclimatised to us, the house, and had had the wire removed from his jaw.

A day or two after this had been done, when Moses was outside the door looking interested, I opened it and stood back. Silvester was on the bed. The ASDIC sounded loudly and he eased himself onto the carpet. Moses had moved into the room with the dignified meander of his maturity. They touched noses and the ASDIC blipped louder than ever. Moses was purring and wafting himself round Silvester's chest. He liked him. It was going to be all right.

The relationship between the two cats bloomed as fast as Silvester's return to health. Within the month he was skittering around after ping-pong balls and engaging Moses in joint washing sessions and silly fights. Soon they could be seen sleeping snuggled up together. Moses' spirit was like a semi-inflated balloon suddenly given the extra air it needed to bounce back and float upward. He was a new cat, like his old self but more so, for he remained closer to us than in Aaron's day, though even years later whenever hot weather came, he was drawn to lie under the laburnum tree.

Silvester treated Nelle like a grumpy granny figure and would tease her till she growled and spat. The more she reacted the better he liked it. For him it was adolescent fun, there was never any malice in it, and she for her part did not dislike him half as much as she pretended, raising no objection to eating her food near him, and occasionally sitting companionably close - well, within a foot or two. She got on with him as well as anyone could have hoped, bearing in mind that she was not a cat person.

Timma liked all cats so long as they had been introduced as legitimate household members, so readily accepted Silvester. I let her see him while I was holding him on my shoulder during the early days of his arrival. He hardly tensed, and she merely registered a new family member.

From then on they seemed to take each other's presence for granted, though he has never been as much of a dog lover as Moses and some of the others.

****

It rapidly became clear that Silvester had the best sense of humour of any cat who has ever lived with us. He was a natural clown, a cartoon cat, who could as meaningfully have had his name spelt with a 'y' as with an 'i'. Life was a joke and nothing seemed to upset him. If he clawed the furniture you could shout discouraging words, bang a newspaper near him, or in desperation (as Graham

104

Haiku (on doors)

Do not think, because
there is a cat flap, you are
excused opening doors.

has been known to do) hurl a magazine in his direction. His response was, and still is, to look over his shoulder, chirrup merrily and continue with the job in paw. Mysteriously, but fortunately, he never actually seems to damage the furniture in these attacks. Perhaps they are mock-ups to tease us, and amuse him.

The living room door is, however, badly mauled. This is our fault, for there is a handle on the larder door which responds to being swung on by Bigfoot. He reasonably expects that all doors will succumb to similar treatment, even when round-handled. He waits till we have just sat down with a post-prandial cup of coffee then launches a barrage which forces one of us to get up for him. He strolls chirpily into the room to seek a lap. Silvester, unlike most cats, never takes offence if you cannot stay still for long. Lifted from your lap, he'll wait for you to settle down again, either in that spot or some other where he's tracked you down, but he draws the line at being carried about. It makes him feel silly, and Silvester has dignity as well as humour. He is very capable of using the cat-flap system, but if I am anywhere near the back door he expects me to open it for him.

****

Silvester would dearly have liked to be a hunter, but unfortunately for him, his injuries left him too slow off the mark. He watches the starlings as they busy about the roof, with his tail lashing and indignant mouthings from the bathroom indoor windowsill, which makes a good hide, but is hardly the best place from which to launch a serious attack. After we had the loft boarded, and began to make regular sorties up there for suitcases, old books and Christmas decorations, whenever we did so he would materialise from the airing cupboard, the kitchen, the garden, almost out of thin air, for his sixth sense was telling him that here was fun. He knew that once up in the loft he was much nearer the scuttering on the roof...maybe starlings even got into the loft sometimes. Silvester certainly did, disappearing into the darkest recesses with no intention of coming out again until he was good and ready. This could be annoying if you wanted to shut the loft and couldn't because of a pot-holing cat. Moreover it was not unknown for him to slip up there unseen and to get trapped for a few hours, emerging cheerful as ever once his protests had secured his release. These days, loft-climbing is prefaced by checking Silvester's whereabouts first, and firmly shutting him in another room, or out on the balcony or anywhere whence we can be sure he cannot effect a clandestine sneak up the ladder.

Out in the open, he made many fruitless lunges in his early days with us, but the only remote successes he had were after other people's mice or birds, and frankly, he lacked the killer instinct. After a while he decided that he'd never really been interested in that sort of thing anyway, and gave up, going in for practising his purr and a shoe fetish instead, for Silvester loves shoes. His favourites are men's size leather - the newer the better - to roll around on, savouring the delicious aroma and texture. He has never scratched a pair of shoes, batting them around with the gloves on, tucking his own massive feet well inside them. I suppose if we were truly caring people we would have a huge leather shoe made for him to call his own. One in which he could snuggle to sleep. As it is he has to make do with lying on our bed. It is a rare event to wake either in the middle of the night or with the alarm in the morning, not to find Silvester comfortably settled between us.

However you look at it, whether or not you give Silvester credit for it (as I like to do) the beginning of 1984 signalled a change for the better in our family life and for events to settle down to normal in the neighbourhood.

Silvester's purr practice brought results. Slowly it began to reappear; erratic at first but then stronger, until after a few months on his good days it would pass the Feline Standard Purr Test. Even now it can have its off days, when it becomes rustily non-existent again, but generally speaking he can be very pleased with his tenacity. He has never lost the talent for loud chirruping, and was able to put this into good use in March of the next year when we moved into even numbers.

Chapter 21

White as a Soul

There is a theory for cats as there is for children that three is not a good number. We did not have the chance to test it on the children as we stopped at two, but we had never found it a problem with the cats, though it was true that Nelle tended to keep herself to herself and her humans. Now we were about to experience what it did to relationships when there were four cats in the household.

Over the previous few years I had made a close friend of Maureen. She worked at Manchester Airport and had rescued several stray cats from there, managing to build relationships with the most feral of them. She was quiet as a cat herself, gentle, with purring eyes and found the hurly-burly of work at the airport less and less to her taste. It seemed worth it however, when one day she had the excitement of rescuing a beautiful white cat with green eyes and a powerful personality, quite different to the usual waif.

Maureen brought her elderly, frail-looking but stalwart mother to lunch when the cat's arrival was so fresh, that a name still had to be chosen. My mother was there too, and the four of us spent an hour or more avidly suggesting possible (and impossible) names for this Elizabeth Taylor of the cat world: 'Snowdrop', 'Snow-white', 'Snowflake', 'Fleur', 'Flower', 'Angel', 'Circe', 'Aphrodite', 'Emerald', and so on. Not surprisingly no decision was reached that day, though 'Daisy' may well have been mentioned. A day or two later Maureen rang to say she had settled on 'Daisy May', and invited me over to meet her.

She was indeed bewitching. Daisy-white, lithely slender, green eyes glowing with affection and arrogance, her sparkling form was trimmed with a little red collar and a bell that tinkled as she moved. 'Tinkerbelle' or 'Bella' would also have suited her, for she was magical. Daisy May, like Nelle, was a people's cat, she would never have chosen to leave a loving home, yet had she been mistreated she would surely have not been so immediately trusting. How she came to be a stray has remained a mystery but she certainly settled into life with Maureen, her mother and the other cats very happily, though she made it clear she expected star treatment. Modesty was not one of her failings!

****

A few months after Daisy May's arrival, Maureen managed at last to organise her exit from the odd hours and frenetic activity of the airport. She wanted more time for home, the garden, the cats, and to give to her mother. She also had plans to become more directly involved with conservation projects, maybe seeking part-time work in that field. The first step was to have a good break, to make space to renew her energies and to take decisions. She went to Australia to stay with her sister, their home set in bush landscape near Melbourne. Maureen loved the place and planned to stay several weeks giving herself time to plan the next stage in her life.

Alas, it was decided for her. Her sister and husband returned from a Saturday morning shopping trip to find Maureen lying in the garden. She had suffered an aneurysm and would have died instantly. She was forty-seven.

****

Maureen had bought the family house from her mother with the intention of looking after her in it. Now this elderly lady, who gave the appearance of being fragile as an autumn leaf, vulnerable to the first puff of cold wind, was left to cope with a large house, garden and four cats. Maureen's mother, Marjorie, was much more than she appeared, however. She had survived not just icy winds, but hurricanes in her life which would have destroyed many people. With the help and support of her other children and her friends, she began coping with this latest earthquaking cruelty.

Of course, I wanted to help, but felt almost guilty when it came to it, for the way in which I could help most, was also of direct benefit to me. Three of the cats, Gracie, Molly, and Ernie (Big Ern) were elderly themselves. They needed to stay with Marjorie as much as she needed them to be with her, but Daisy May was a different set of paws. She was young, only two to three years old, and she was too adventurous for her own good. Marjorie had seen her more than once on the other side of the murderous main road. Maureen would have been horrified. And so it was that I got the phone call asking whether we could offer Daisy May a home.

I was pleased and touched by the offer. Daisy May was a dazzling cat, but I also felt that in some way I would be keeping in touch with Maureen, making her loss a little easier to bear. I conferred with Graham, of course, and he not only understood the way I felt, but recognised that there was about as much chance of our not having Daisy May, as there had been of not having Sam all those years ago.

****

It was a day in March when I travelled like a kidnapper with my wicker cat basket. I did not stay long. It was an emotional moment and for everyone's sake it seemed better to take Daisy May quickly and get her safey installed in our spare bedroom. She was not pleased to find herself trapped in a basket, and much less pleased to find herself travelling in a car. She protested very loudly. However, she greeted me cordially enough when I opened up the cat basket and seemed not to disapprove of her temporary quarters. She must have been relieved that the ordeal by vehicle was over, for this affable initial mood did not last long. After all, she had been catnapped from a perfectly satisfactory home, thank you very much, only to be confined in a comfortable but crampingly restrictive space for a cat of her talents. She was miffed.

Daisy May was a star, a prima donna, she expected to be respected as such. She was visibly more frosty with me on the second day of her confinement, and when I stroked her and suggested picking her up for a cuddle, she took a swipe at me and drew blood. It was the only time I have ever been scratched spitefully by any of our cats, but it was to happen on two further occasions with Daisy May. I was upset, not by the wounds, for I'd received far worse from over-enthusiastic play on other occasions from other claws, but because I wanted her to be happy, and she plainly was not. My patient explanations cut no ice with the Snow Queen.

I had been going to keep her in for two weeks, and I spent as much time as I could with her inside the spare room, while Silvester took up guard duty outside the door. The asdic chirrup came into its own over this period. He would sit on the landing for hours serenading Daisy through the door. On her side, she would sniff the feline minstrel under the barricade, and glare at me in disgust for not giving her her freedom.

After about ten days, I could stand it no longer and decided to risk letting her out. Silvester was ecstatic, and asdicked into the room to greet her. Daisy May responded with an affronted hiss, which did not put Silvester out in the least. She eschewed his overtures and began taking the air in the rest of the house. Moses she accepted as the senior citizen, besides he did not thrust his attentions on her, his greeting was friendly but not intimate. And Nelle? Both she and Moses had been very aware of Daisy's presence in the spare bedroom, they had come to know her scent and had been expecting to meet her in due course. Nelle looked down from her perch on the record player where she was listening to Schubert, flicked her tail, wrinkled her pink nose, and bided her time. She came to the conclusion that she was pleased to have a female in the camp to balance the men, and she and Daisy May were to develop a friendly rapport, and could often be seen sitting near one another or greeting one another in a pleased manner. Each of them preferred people (and Timma) to cats, but if it had to be a cat then make it female.

Once Daisy May had the run of the house it was going to be impossible to keep her inside, with everybody else coming and going through the catflap, so within an hour of her release from the spare room she had achieved the freedom of outdoors. It was a terrifying moment, for now she could choose whether she wanted to stay with us. She had just walked across the lawn to examine the first of the cherry trees, when the friend who had moved into Hazel's old house, appeared at the front gate with her huge Bernese Mountain Dog. They were greeted by a loud cry implying, "Go Away!" with the hasty explanation "I've just let Daisy May out!" Fortunately, Verity was one to take life in her stride, was fond of cats, knew about Daisy May and could instantly understand my vision of her disappearing back towards Manchester, having been panicked by the lunge of an elephantine dog. Quietly they faded, leaving me to track Daisy May round the garden, which was not difficult as white is hardly the colour for spring camouflage, and the chinking of her bell gave her presence away, even when out of sight.

It was a warm day, a good day for a thorough recky, and she was thorough, exploring almost every tree, trunk to top, and climbing her way onto the roof of the house to be found protesting on the spare room window ledge that she could not get in. Having completed her assessment, Daisy May decided that so long as outdoors was part of the deal, this was a desirable place to be and she would condescend to grace us permanently with her presence.

It was a warmish spring that year and one day I was planting some shrub roses in the lawn to soften the effect of the brick of the new garage. Her bell chinking, Daisy May came winding her way through the clumps of daffodils to offer help, a comforting purr and thrust of her head against my hand. She was never vicious with me again once she was set free, though she can be irra-tionally ratty, courting affection one moment then giving a "Myick!" of dis-approval the next, accompanied with a claws-in pat and maybe a nibble. This kind of behaviour she particularly enjoys inflicting on Graham or any visiting man. She likes men, but thinks they should be kept in their place. Surprisingly, she is also keen on small children and babies, unlike any of our other cats. When visiting children come, she is pleased to see them, and likes to get on the mother's knee with the baby!

She was also delighted when we had a white rabbit to stay. We were looking after him for friends while they were on holiday, and Daisy seemed to think he was there to amuse her. She would sit beside his run, or perch like a tea cosy

Haiku (on being beautiful)

I can make her smile
when she is sad, by being
simply beautiful.

on top of it, while Pasty tried to touch noses through the wire, welcoming the company. I have known of rabbits and cats forming close friendships and if Pasty had been staying longer, or I had been a little braver it would have been interesting to see how they got on without the safety device of the wire netting. It was a special relationship between the rabbit and one cat, none of the others took any notice at all.

I have been asked more than once whether Daisy May is deaf, as there is a common belief that all pure white cats are thus afflicted, unless they have unmatching eyes. Daisy has perfectly matched green eyes that turn to emeralds at night, and she is as alert to sound as the keenest hunter. She never appeared irritated by her collar and bell, but rarely caught anything despite her patience in the field. Maureen had fitted all her cats with bells to reduce the likelihood of them catching birds, and Daisy had the additional handicap of her colour, attractive to white rabbits but a goodly warning to wildlife.

After a year or so, on the advice of the vet I removed the collar, as he said he had seen too many nasty accidents happen to cats in collars, even those which like Daisy's were elasticated. I think she missed it a little, and we certainly found it strange that Daisy May could now silently materialise without warning. She was not quite so keen on hunting by this time - maybe she'd been discouraged by the bell for too long, but apart from one or two mice, her level of catch did not increase.

I missed Daisy May in her red collar, she looked so pretty in it, as well she knew, for she was very vain; beautiful enough to compete in any cat show I told her. It would never have occurred to me, of course, to take her to one, but nonetheless it may have been that vague thought which prodded me into going to see what a cat show was like, when there was a small one held at our local leisure centre. It is an irony that the first cat show, organised by Harrison Weir in 1871, was held with the intent of bettering the lot of cats, to try to change people's attitude, so that they accepted, liked, and welcomed cats into their homes as much as they already welcomed dogs.

I did not know this when I made my brief afternoon excursion, and I am afraid it reinforced every prejudice I have ever had about breeding animals for show, and indeed the ethics of showing at all. It felt wrong to see cats sitting in cages primped with satin frills, waiting to be judged on the precise shape of eyes, or tail tip or whether their body was sufficiently "typey." This was a way of massaging the egos of the cats' owners, which seemed to me as degrading for the cats as beauty contests are for women, though at least, one presumes, the women can choose whether or not to take part.

I came away determined never to go to another cat show, and told Daisy May all about it. She entirely agreed that the principle of judging was wrong, remarking that a cat is a cat, not an ornament and that their natural skills and full personality cannot possibly be assessed in the artificial setting of a show. Moreover, their best secrets are mysteries they keep to themselves.

Chapter Twenty Two

Mysterious and Blue

Other animals have mysteries too. In order that Daisy May should not lose contact with her old friend, I would sometimes drive over to Bramhall and bring Marjorie back here for lunch or tea. One morning I was on one of these missions, when coming round the bend of a narrowish but busy country road I was surprised to find drivers weaving their way round a dog, standing dazed in the middle of the traffic, apparently oblivious to it. It did not take a great deal of intelligence to surmise that here was an accident waiting to happen. Another driver, a young Scotsman coming from the other direction had surmised the same and we both converged on the dog, who was a brown mix-up with a roughish curly coat who seemed helplessly rooted to his parking spot. He was vaguely pleased to talk to me, and not knowing what on earth else to do I invited him into my car. The young Scotsman asked, "What are you going to do with him?" I replied with all the confidence of my mature years, "I haven't a clue." We agreed though, that the first step was to ensure that there remained a dog to do something with, and he wished me luck and we drove off in our respective directions.

Timma was very possessive of her vehicle for all her mild temperament. There had been an occasion some years before when taking a car to be assessed for trade-in, I had airily said to the salesman, "Oh by the way the dog's in the car, but there's no need to worry about her," adding with a laugh, "She won't bite." He came back minutes later looking visibly shaken, holding his hand and saying with a rueful grin, "I thought you said...." Not one of my more glorious moments.

This anecdote came to mind as I encouraged my new found friend into the car, half expecting Timma to take huge exception to the intrusion. She was politeness itself, however, maybe sensing that here was someone in trouble, and off we set, an unplanned threesome. We stopped several times to ask if anyone knew, or knew of, my passenger, but drew a blank, so Marjorie was greeted by a car with two dogs in it, not that she minded, being as concerned for his safety as I was, and my unplanned passenger seemed rather to enjoy the ride alongside Timma on the back seat.

It remained a problem what to do about him. I made all the usual phone calls with no joy; he was wearing a collar but no disc. I took him to the vet for a checkup, who said he was around thirteen or fourteen and very deaf, otherwise he was in good health. That night after a good meal, he slept the sleep of the worn-out in the back room of our garage where we had made him up a bed. Graham was not keen on taking in "another of your waifs and strays," and our local, excellent animal sanctuary, was full to the gunnels. My parents said they would ask Cindy what she thought about offering him a home there, and she being the magnanimous dog that she was, said, "Yes, why not?"

My mother said afterwards, that it was like having a perfectly behaved guest to stay. He was no trouble, but she could sense that he was never totally relaxed. About three weekends later, when we were away, the inevitable happened. My father went out to the garage for something and left the front door open. The dog slipped past him and was off, moving at speed. My father got the car out and tried to follow him but it was hopeless, and my parents spent a miserable and worried evening, and a restless tormented night. Their one hope was that this time he was wearing a disc marked with their name and address.

At seven-thirty on the Saturday morning the phone rang and a voice said, "I believe you may have been looking after our dog." Strider, for that was his name, had lost his disc on the last day of his owners' holiday in Anglesey.

On returning to Cheadle next day, it was high on their agenda to get him a new one, but while they were visiting their daughter he had mysteriously vanished from the front garden. He had never done anything like it before, and they had no knowledge of his being deaf. Their frantic phone calls had drawn blanks as mine had done, not saying a great deal for co-ordination between the agencies concerned.

No one quite knew what to make of his untypical behaviour, but if he had suffered some sort of brainstorm and become doolally for a while, on recovering himself he had made the most magnificent return, covering eight or ten miles to his own door, over an unknown terrain, dangerous with roads and traffic. His owners were ecstatic to have him back, and later that Saturday morning a huge bouquet of flowers arrived for my parents: "From Strider - with love."

****

Daisy May had been with us about a year when we found the need for a London cat. A house belonging to my mother had had the same sitting tenant for about sixty years. The rent had hardly covered the cost of repairs, but the elderly lady who lived in it was happy there, in fact we think she believed she owned it, so there was no question of disturbing her. At last, in her mid-eighties she died, leaving the house a highly saleable commodity, for it was boom time and prices rising with each day. My mother generously decided that the proceeds from the sale should go to my sister and to me.

Graham and I had often said when away on holiday, "Wouldn't it be lovely to have a little cottage here?" (Scotland), "Or here?" (Corsica) "Or here?" (Cornwall). I suppose most people have played these games, but when faced with the chance to make it come true, there are a lot of pros and cons to weigh up; caring for a home at a distance, being tied to that one place for all or most future holidays, the hassle involved if you decide to let it, and so on. Some of our friends were astonished when we decided that our retreat should be in central London, but it had many advantages, not least that Graham's work took him down there at least once a week, and that we both liked London, enjoying the range of theatres, cinemas, art galleries, concerts, etc. It would also give us a chance to see friends in the South more often.

As expected, the house sold quickly, and the trick was to buy almost simultaneously, before flat prices outstripped what we could afford. We gave ourselves one weekend to find something, and as with Throstles' Nest struck lucky. We must have viewed nine or ten properties, some, said to be "highly desirable studio flats" consisted of one room hardly the size of a small garage, with a cooker tucked in a corner that was imaginatively described as "the kitchen." Others were bigger, but in an institutionalised block, or secreted five floors up in an elegant-from-outside tall white period property (whose tatty stairways smelt of stale cabbage and school dinners) with no lift.

Our lucky stumble was away from Chelsea and Notting Hill Gate and into Camden Town. The flat we found was in a Georgian terrace backing onto the Grand Union Canal. The house had just been converted into four flats and the one on the first floor, which we liked best, was still for sale.

Of course it was small, furnishing it was like playing at houses, but it had a reasonable size sitting/dining area with a pleasant L-shape for the kitchen, a bathroom with a proper window to outdoors, and a short corridor leading to a bedroom overlooking the canal, giving a feeling of space that is a rare commodity in London.

The Saturday we moved in, we were struggling to install two large sofa beds that only just made it round the curve of the stair, when we met the couple who were going to live above us; they were shifting a piano at the time, helped by their Border Collie who was a working dog, building a career in computer software alongside her owners.

We were glad that there was a built-in dog on the premises, but we were without a cat. I put a collage of photos in the corridor which helped a bit, but it still did not feel entirely like home. It took a while to solve the problem, but you can get almost anything in the market at Camden Lock and at last I found her: an Egyptian goddess painted deep blue on papyrus. The Egyptians held cats to be sacred and the cat-headed goddess Bastet, was revered as a symbol of fertility. I once read somewhere that a corruption of her name has led to our modern expression of 'pussycat', but I am not sure I am convinced.

We called our deep blue cat 'Papyrus' and enthroned her in a dark wooden frame. Fresh flowers are not a practical proposition for our brief sojourns, so we have always made do with dried ones and bowls of sweetly scented pot-pourri, changed on each visit. One of these bowls is placed in front of Papyrus, looking like an offering, and at night I leave my rings and earrings cushioned on its fragrant contents, as if in her safe-keeping.

Thinking back to all the mystic powers invested in cats by the Egyptians, it is easy to imagine that when she has the place to herself, Papyrus steps from her frame, growing to full cat size as she does so and enjoying an elegant roll on the Persian rug. She peacefully survived, or protected us from our one burglar, who left cleanly and swiftly on finding our flat furnished with near-antique video and stereo equipment, and a neanderthal black and white television. The only thing he could find to tempt him was a pair of large leather gloves, and maybe he only took those to help him hide his fingerprints on the next job.

****

The spring of the year had brought us the fun of the flat and acquiring our London cat, but what goes up with the swings must come down with the roundabouts. Cindy had made a graceful exit in September and Timma was now fifteen. All through the year she had been growing frailer. Her eyesight was failing and in the evenings she wandered restlessly, showing that insufficient oxygen was getting to the brain. By the autumn her legs were beginning to give way now and again, and on one occasion she slipped down from the drive into the deep gulley which surrounds the old part of the house. It would soon be time to say goodbye, and we all dreaded it. It was noticeable that all the cats made an extra fuss of her, rubbing gently round her as she stood looking bemused, and the boys found it hard to come to terms with life without her. Harry was away studying at a sixth form college in Cambridge, and insisted we postpone any action that final week till the Saturday morning, so that he could be there. It was early November, golden as it can sometimes be, and the sun was warm as Harry carried her tenderly halfway up the field and

118

then let her walk (she almost trotted) down again, beside him. She looked laughing and happy, reminding me of that other occasion, when in full health she had arrowed back to me. It is a good memory, in a gentle autumn, the season at its best, the birch leaves flickering against the green of the hill, promising in their dying glow the renewal of growth - and a puppy.

Chapter Twenty Three

The Labradollie

We all wanted a puppy, the family felt incomplete without a dog, but there were three good reasons for a temporary delay. The first was to allow a proper space to grieve for Timma, the second was that we were none of us sure what sort of replacement we wanted, though I was very tempted by the idea of a Malamute. Lastly, we had a ski-ing holiday booked for a week over New Year.

Lest this sound glamorous, the record should be set straight. The previous Easter we had ventured for the first time, gone to Austria, where the only decent snow left was on slopes which felt to me like the north face of the Eiger. Ski-ing seemed to be an uncomfortable and terrifying business, involving clomping long distances with iron weights on your feet, frantically attempting to scramble on (and worse still, off) bits of moving wire with saddles like coat hangers, and being berated by a ludicrously supple instructor who had been on skis before he was out of nappies. He could not understand why we (particularly me) found it so difficult, and I could hardly explain to him that, like Timma, my only response to being bellowed at, was to shrivel up inside and fail to achieve anything, so that his ever fiercer cries of *"NO, NO, NO, Diana, bend zee kneez, bend zee kneez!"* were as wasted as if hurled in Hindustani. Moreover, my name is not Diana.

Hugo, of course, was soon swooping around with all the irritating confidence of the young, even if his style was eccentric. Harry was an old hand, a black-run off-piste man, who was tolerantly amused at his parents pathetic efforts. The pièce de disaster came on the last morning. The previous afternoon had been spent in almost private tuition on gentler slopes. Everyone else in our group had the schuss and parallel turns sussed and had gone off to practice, with depressing competence. The instructor, left with the two older and more inept learners, had stopped shouting, and I was getting used to being called Diana, so that I felt I gained more in that last session than in all the rest of the week put together. Ski-ing was close to becoming enjoyable.

The last morning dawned in thick mist, a suitable setting for a Stephen King horror story. The boys were not in the least daunted, and set off for some ambitious bit of mountain, of which Graham and I would have been wary in full sunlight. It was no place to risk in a white-out. We unadventurously made our way to familiar territory and successfully put into practice all that we had learned the day before. During the last half-hour or so, the boys - having "done" their mountain - came to have a laugh on ours, and their mother put on a special giggle for them; convinced I was almost at the bottom of a steep slope, I launched confidently into a schuss expecting the natural flattening of the ground to slow me down, as indeed it would have done had I been anywhere near my target. In fact I must have been more than halfway up, travelling downward, faster, faster, ever faster into a threat of white, only the rise of panic outpacing my skis. In a flash of inspiration I forgot every damned thing I thought I had learnt, and with huge presence of mind fell head first into a degrading heap, one ski sticking loyally to my foot, the other disowning me and disappearing into the loathsome murk.

I escaped with a banged head, bruised pride and the determination that down-hill ski-ing was not for me, despite any comfort my menfolk could manage between badly concealed smiles. But Hugo had caught the ski-ing bug and wanted to go again the next season, so we hit on a compromise. We would go to Bulgaria for New Year, where those who wanted to downhill could, and the rest could try cross-country.

This was much more like it. It felt like a holiday and not an outward bound course. The boots are soft as slippers, there are no coat hangers to worry about, the slopes are gentle, and if you fall over it's a cushioned tumble into soft pow-dered snow. True you have to propel yourself much of the time, but you feel in control. The forest was quiet, and so was the instructor, and there were only four or five of us in the group. The morning ended with mulled wine in the hut where the ski-slippers lived, then the rest of the day was ours to relax as we wanted. We enjoyed this holiday, and apparently the downhill wasn't bad either.

****

To return to choosing a puppy: the Malamute was used by the Inuits as a sled dog, and is the closest canine relation to the wolf, an animal for which I have a soft spot as having been badly maligned by the vicious fiction of fairy tale. Malamutes, like wolves, do not bark but look at you with that downward thrust of the head so typical of the wolf, and it was this same gaze, round the corner of a house where I was collecting for the Worldwide Fund for Nature, that won my heart, especially when the huge threatening animal advanced on me, only to lean affectionately against my knees. I wanted one. However, they are not altogether easy dogs to manage, and the more we went into it, the more it did not seem very sensible, for us as a family. I still had guilt feelings too, about having succumbed to having pedigree cats, so with considerable regret the Malamute idea was rejected.

I talked to the vet, we consulted as a family, but it was my mother who spotted the advertisement in the local paper and showed it to Hugo. A farm out in the hills had "First cross Labrador with Border Collie puppies". Hugo persuaded me to go, "just to have a look." Even I am not so stupid as to think it likely we would come away without securing a prize. We didn't. We were done for the moment we arrived. All eight of them were enchanting cuddly rolypolies, five were black with a bit of white here and there, three were gold. From the depths of genetics, gold can occur out of two black parents, and it was the gold that Hugo favoured. I left the choice up to him, explained that we would be away in Bulgaria until 4th January, and paid a deposit of £5. This was on the heavy side, as the total price for our expensive designer puppy was £7.50p. She would be barely seven weeks old on our return from holiday, but we were assured she would be ready to leave her mother, a smooth-coated Border Collie with an affectionate nature.

****

The news of our rash commitment had to be broken to the rest of the family. Harry was not sure; he had been keen on the Malamute idea, a Labradollie sounded a bit tame to him, and anyway we should have chosen a black one. Graham as usual, said he left all major family decisions to me, and if I was happy, so was he. My mother took the credit for spotting the advertisement. The cats could hardly be expected to welcome a rombustious interloper, when they had become used to being a happy band of four.

****

Moses, Nelle, Silvester, Daisy May. Each different in character, each with a different relationship to the other three:

Moses still had the widest beat, and even after Silvester's arrival, was prone to inexplicable character change. In warm weather if he was not to be found under the laburnum tree he could be missing for long hours, sunning himself in some remote corner of a neighbour's garden. Once, he went through a patch of several months where he confined himself to a box in the utility room, hardly coming through into the house at all, and this was long after he was secure in Silvester's affection. They were devoted to each other, but Silvester, like Aaron before him, was a short-haul cat, always well within earshot, and the first to arrive if I was ever calling anyone else. Having been self-ostracised, Moses then took a huge fancy to the airing cupboard over the winter, and could often be found in there snuggled up to his best friend. Moses got on well with Nelle and Daisy May, but it was a slightly distant relationship, as it was with us sometimes, though the older he got the more affectionate he became.

Silvester continued to be the clown who liked to be liked by everyone, but unable to resist teasing the girls, which inevitably produced much hissing and spitting. He gradually relented with Nelle, maybe recognising that she was older, and not in the best of health. He adored Daisy May, often wanting to play, but she was usually disdainful and would reject his advances, spit and rush off. As soon as she did this, he went galumphing after her. He remained the least soft-footed cat I have ever known. Down in the kitchen, you could hear a mighty thump that told you he had left the airing cupboard in the bathroom above, or a sound like marauding elephants would betray silly fights with Moses or the teasing of Daisy May. To hear his thunderous footfalls, you would expect to meet a monster cat, but he never put on much weight, despite all attempts, he remained rangy.

Nelle, with her pink nose, was devoted as ever, and a neat little helper. She did not obstruct tasks in hand, but would sit companionably alongside or on a lap, whereas Daisy May had to be in the middle of any activity, stomping all over the letter I was writing, or thrusting herself in my line of vision, so that I misdialled telephone numbers, or taking over the typing with coded messages of her own. She drew the line at cooking however, while Nelle favoured the stove. It was electric, with coiled rings that remained warm for a good while when switched off. Nelle would perch on the edge of the stove hazardously close to the ring, either enjoying the actual warmth, or in the hope that she could influence it to radiate in her direction. She had another spot entirely hers, in a tiny nook on the landing where no other cat has gone. She was small enough to curl comfortably between a stair and the wall eight inches away, and under the carpet ran the hot pipes to the radiator. She was a diviner of warmth, but I worried about her when we came to eradicate the last of the orange formica. When the kitchen was refurbished I would dearly have liked a stove with a ceramic hob, but was afraid she might not realise how it could burn, being used to coiled hotplates. For Nelle's sake I chose to have solid plates on the new stove, which took half an hour to bring water to the boil and eventually drove us to gas!

The cats were not keen on their kitchen being pulled apart, but there was a moment of celebration when the large pine worktop was installed. It was glowing with protective layers of poly this and that, but it was wide and long and new. It had to be inspected by the full team. It was the only time I had been able to take a photograph of Moses, Nelle, Silvester and Daisy May all together, but there they all were, deciding that maybe the upheaval had been worthwhile, for here was a surface they could be proud of and comfortable on. There would be one other occasion in the future when they would all gather in this same place.

****

All the cats had been fond of Timma, especially Moses and Nelle, but a quiet elderly lady is hardly the same thing as the riotous toddler who burst upon them with indecent haste on our return from Bulgaria. The boys could not wait to unpack their bags before the puppy was paramount. My plans, allowing twenty-four hours for re-entry and checking we had the layette prepared were swept aside.

Next morning we were off to collect the dog with no name, for we could not agree. Graham and I had wanted to call her 'Sofia', after the capital of Bulgaria. This was viewed as "silly" and "twee" by our sons but they could not think of a name they liked themselves. We thought that when we saw her again the problem might resolve itself.

It was three weeks since Hugo and I had seen her, and we could not avoid the cliché. "Haven't you *grown?*" I said to her. Harry looked embarrassed, either at his mother's obvious remark, or because he could not disguise the rush of affection he unexpectedly felt towards this new and adorable woman in his life. She appeared to be a happy bustly little bundle of a person, but she was about to be wrenched from everyone she knew. We all felt for her, as I handed over the massive balance of £2.50p, and Hugo tenderly carried her to the car. He cuddled her on his knee, for Harry, apparently nervous lest he hurt one so small, had opted for his brother to have the privilege.

She had never been in a car before. What did this roaring tin can feel like to her? A huge world was passing by outside, her world of the womb-like barn, with its doggy smells of brothers, sisters, mother and warm straw was gone for-ever. We discussed all this on the homeward journey, convinced ourselves that she would be in major shock and a victim of severe trauma by the time we reached home, and were prepared for problems: She would be off her food, have an upset stomach, cry all night and probably all day, chew the furniture, destroy her box....

Hugo put her gently down on the kitchen floor and she confidently bounced towards Harry. I put down a small meal of tinned meat for her (this was what she was used to) and she gobbled it up. I put her inside a construction I had made to emulate a playpen. Several recent puppy owners had told me how much puppies like to be in a playpen, as the small space makes them feel safe.

I had not had time on our return to get hold of a proper pen, but I thought I was the mother of invention with my effort, made with an old door and various devices dug from the garden shed. The boys had said it was a stupid idea and our nameless puppy demonstrated the point. She put her small shoulder to the construction and shoved enough of it aside to break free. She had ignored the carefully prepared cardboard box padded with soft blankets inside her playpen, and on bustling her way out onto the vast plain of the kitchen floor, she waddled across several acres to drop off to sleep, exhausted, on the cold hard tiles under the pine table.

What a communicator. Who needs words, when your body language is so skilled? I had got it wrong. This small person, the dog with no name, had been born in a barn. What were its features? A cold hard floor, a lowish ceiling, and an even lower level of lighting, plus the companionship of her brothers and sisters. We had scored high on the love and cuddles stakes, but had failed the accommodation test. We had a rethink. The boys removed all evidence of the rejected pen, and I went rummaging under the stairs for a venerable tray on legs which had belonged to my grandparents. I do not know why I had kept it, as it was neither beautiful nor much good as a tray, for it wobbbled alarmingly if anything more than a teabag was rested on it. I cannot claim that I had thought, "One day that will come in really useful," although I have kept many other objects on that premise, and am still waiting for them to justify my optimism.

The tray, however, made a perfect roof over the Labradollie's cardboard box. I draped a towel over the top for extra cover, and when she woke up, played and was tired again, she settled contentedly, apparently satisfied that she now had her own private barn.

She was barely seven weeks old, so we had to expect puddles.

It meant keeping her mainly in the kitchen, where the tiles could be easily wiped clean. This gave rise to a problem. If we shut the door through to the dining room, then the cats would have their free run of the house curtailed, which would be very unpopular. The answer was a Mothercare gate, set firmly across the gap at the end of the kitchen before the small passage to the dining room door. It had to be cleverer than that, for our Labradollie was small enough to squeeze through between the bars. Chicken wire was the solution, and even my sons were impressed with this idea. There remained a slight problem. The cats, of course, could leap onto and then over the gate, but they had to make a brief pause before take-off and on landing. The Labradollie saw this as a hilarious game, the object of which was to bounce on a passing cat with friendly enthusiasm. The cats were not keen on this sport, but found they were stuck with it, for she was not in the least deterred by their protestations, and the referee found it very difficult to blow the whistle on what was harmless fun. The cats did not dislike her, they seemed glad to have a dog about the place again, if only she would stop bouncing. She did, more or less, for one day the gate got dislodged and fell to the floor with a terrifying clatter. The Labradollie disappeared into the safety of her barn, and did not go near the gate again for years afterwards.

****

For two days we struggled to find a name, 'Sofia' or 'Sophie' having been ruled out. So were 'Goldie', 'Honey', 'Blanche' (after her white tail tip) 'Jan', 'Dollie', 'Elsa', and all subsequent suggestions. We were not doing well, and it was becoming ridiculous not being able to call our puppy anything but "Good girl." Fortunately, Marion next-door came to the rescue, she took one look and in her warm Scottish voice said, "Have you not thought of 'Rosie'?" I thought it was perfect and kicked myself for having forgotten that if Hugo had been a girl, I had intended to call him Rosanna - 'Rosie' for short. I waited for the boys to say, "Oh NO! Soppy! Boring!" But they didn't, for it is surely a recognised fact that suggestions never sound as silly coming from other people's mothers as from your own. The family was agreed; at last the Labradollie had a name and we could address her with proper decorum.

Chapter Twenty Four

Not Rosie All The Way

As a child I used to hate January and February, for they were the big let-down after Christmas before the spring brought my birthday. In later years I have come to agree with T.S.Eliot that "April is the cruellest month..." for spring often comes in name only, an impostor, blasting hailstones, sleeting bitter gusts at the hosts of struggling daffodils, reaching chilling fingers into our bones, depressing spirits in need of sunny respite by the time the clocks move forward. I do not mind how cold it is during winter, and I will remain cheerful through the worst March winds, but I expect some warmth the next month, and year after year it disappoints, dropping me in the April blues.

January on the other hand provides a welcome lull after the demands of December and Christmas. Sometimes I even manage to tidy a couple of the drawers that have been bulging for attention all through the previous year. This particular January was reserved for Rosie. Time and attention lavished on a puppy in the early weeks repays large dividends as your dog matures. At least that's the theory that seems to have worked for us so far. I have never felt the need for rigid training programmes that subjugate the dog's personality to that of the owner, I like to see dogs' characters develop as fully as possible, but that should not mean that they are badly behaved or a nuisance to other people. I would not want the responsibility of owning a vicious or uncontrollable animal. This is a good reason for starting with a puppy and having some vague idea of the temperament to expect.

****

Rosie's first January was deep with snow, through which she floundered and romped, almost disappearing into its cold softness. Marion called her 'Rosie Butterball' as she rolled golden in the whiteness, and Jossie, Marion's leggy black Labrador hardly out of puppyhood herself could not contain her excitement; injections or no injections she was going to play with Rosie. She burst through the hedge and nearly flattened our puppy with exuberance. Rosie was not remotely daunted and a firm friendship was cemented.

Being new to winter and to life in general, Rosie assumed snow was normal and there for the pleasure of it. She had a great capacity for enjoyment, and she and I made the most of it. There were days when going out anywhere was nearly impossible and everything drew to a cosy silence of white, which reinforced the plan to give our puppy maximum attention. It enhanced our feeling of closeness as she responded to all the toys we had gathered for her, attacking an old football, dribbling it with skill and sharp teeth till it gave in. Deflated, it allowed itself to be shaken to death. She chewed on the marrow bones provided for her and never on furniture or our shoes or even her own cardboard bed, where she cuddled up with her 'dolly' a baggily soft toy dog that Hugo had purchased at a school fair years before for two or three pence.

Rosie rapidly became used to the idea that what goes out must come back home again. At first I would leave her for only half an hour, gradually increasing the length of time so that she grew confident of my eventual return. She came to take it in her stride if left at home for several hours, though she also became a good car traveller. Nervous of the car at first, I got her used to it by taking her on very short journeys, literally just driving round the block, with no other purpose than for her to feel safe in this strange machine. She was so small and intimidated that she snuggled on my lap and never moved. We progressed to going to meet Hugo off the school bus, which she found exciting, and gradually she began to enjoy and then to relish car rides. She came to think of the front passenger seat as hers by right. Woe betide anyone who usurps her place; they get heavily leaned on from the rear seat, and generously festooned in golden hair. She enjoys watching the world go by, and seems able to recognise people she knows from long distances.

She always hopes to come with me, but there is a point in the year when some days it is too risky to leave her in the parked car even for short spells because of the oven factor; even with the windows left open the insides of cars can heat more quickly than most cookers. It pays to be very careful, for it can be cool and cloudy when you leave the vehicle and dangerously sunny half an hour later. She seems to understand, and accepts, "Sorry Rosie, not today, it's too hot," as a signal to settle down in the cool of home. It is one of my nightmares to return to the car to find an expiring dog. The other is to return and find no car; having your car stolen is not much fun, but it is a positive party compared with having it stolen with your dog in it. I would never leave her anywhere considered high risk for car theft.

****

It was not a surprise, but it was nonetheless fascinating to see the two distinctive aspects of Rosie's parentage emerge. She was indeed a Labradollie, with the lively intelligence and indefatigability of the Border Collie, tempered with the gentler nature (and greed) of the Labrador. She learnt very fast, built up a sound vocabulary of words she understood (even when spelt) and has a memory like an elephant for people, places and unpleasant experiences. She never forgave the gate for falling on her, and her bubbling enthusiasm for everyone she met was suddenly disillusioned in some unfathomable way. She is a recklessly agile jumper, and maybe on one of her early sorties over the wall onto the footpath (where her sole aim was to greet every passer-by with rapture) some child or its parent reacted badly and maybe lashed out at her; understandable if they were frightened, but they succeeded in frightening Rosie more. So much so that she has remained terrified of anyone under the age of twelve ever since, and retreats under the nearest available barn when any children visit us. This is rather embarassing, for all the small people involved have been gentleness itself, yet she suffers their caresses with the convincing tremble of someone with a phobia. She is the canine equivalent of people who say, "I know it's silly but I can't help being frightened of all dogs because of a bad experience I had with this huge horrible hairy one when I was four."

It is precisely for that sort of reason that I was determined that she would learn from the beginning never to jump up at people, and would push her rump firmly to the ground when guests arrived. She learnt fast, though when favourite people come, the tail thrashes with the visible effort of keeping her bottom on the ground!

****

It is a big moment when your puppy has had the final protective injection and can go out for that first walk. In our case it was up into the field at the back of the house. Rosie had hardly begun her first gambol when halfway up she spotted someone with a Jack Russell. This was adventure, discovery, and she was off to say hallo. The Jack Russell, whose name was Rex, and his owner who was called Ann, were enchanted by this small burst of happiness, and the two dogs played until they were exhausted. Rex was like a clockwork toy that had been wound up, he circled low and fast through the grass. Rosie was still bouncing, which slowed her down a bit, but a good time was had by all. She never forgot Ann or Rex as a result of that morning, and they often used to take her for an extra walk when they were passing our door. It got to the stage where you could not say the name "Ann" even in a conversational tone about someone quite different, without Rosie's ears pricking up and an expectant look at the door. Moreover, sometimes on a journey miles from home, I would notice someone with white hair who reminded me vaguely of Ann, and would then sense Rosie beside me stiffening, and staring with devoted intensity.

****

A Labradollie is a very different creature to take for a walk from a Terrier. Rosie had no hunting instincts at all, apart from the need to be constantly retrieving a stick. She has trained us into the rhythm of this, but it is not quite so easy to sort your thoughts or lines for the next masterpiece when you are on incessant stick duty. It is like having an invisible lead, so in areas where it says, "Dogs on leads, or under strict control," we never need worry. Our dog is invisibly bonded to the path of her stick: she follows it, retrieves and expects it thrown again; if it is not she barks with the determined energy of the Collie. There is never the slightest chance of her being out of vision. She will occasionally make a vague lunge in the direction of rabbits, but she rapidly learnt that there is no point because they move too fast, and anyway one's hope of catching anything is more than a little restricted by having a large stick in one's mouth, the larger the better. There was one notable exception to this in some Northumbrian sand dunes, where she was for once sniffing a hole. Out popped a baby rabbit and in its panic leaped into Rosie's amazed mouth. It was not clear who was the more surprised or terrified by the experience, but she responded instantly to "Rosie drop!" The rabbit's scut blinked back down the hole.

Several people have told us horror stories about dogs impaled on sticks or getting them stuck in their throats, pouring blood. It is easy to make a misthrow and this can lead to danger; we have been lucky so far, the worst our misthrows have done is to lose sticks up trees. We have always chosen our sticks very carefully, trying to avoid any that could be potentially dangerous. It would also appear that certain woods taste more delicious than others. Dead gorse and larch are two flavours of the month. Sticks are a serious business, there are times in the year when a decent one becomes a rarity, other incongruous occasions (like walking across one of the islands of The Great Barrier Reef) when we see a veritable stick mine and find it hard not to gather them, stuff them in our suitcases and bring them back in triumph. Then there is the mystery of The Sinker. Why, sometimes, does an apparently dry, light stick, sink forever into the depths of the reservoir, leaving Rosie swimming in forlorn searching circles, when a heavier number responds by bobbing amicably on the surface?

Whereas Timma would venture into water only if the weather was truly hot, Rosie has proved to be a waterbaby. Part of her daily routine is a swim in the reservoir. She hurls herself into the water in Olympic belly flops, retrieving her baton. Then it's drop, shake and start again - unless we have had the bad luck to pick a Sinker. She will want to swim no matter how cold the weather, so it is up to us to impose a veto, if the winds are too Siberian, or if there is ice beginning to form on the surface. We always give her a good rub down with a warm towel on getting home anyway, as I naively hope this may be a guard against arthritis as she grows older. I suppose I am conscious of this danger as she broke her leg when she was six months old - mainly through over-enthusiastic play - for she skittered into some hot ash left on the reservoir bank by fisherman who had been "making improvements" and fell a few feet from a shelf which projects over a doorway in the bank, housing some controls for the water level. It gave us all a fright, but did not calm her down for long.

To my horror, less than a week later she leapt over the lower half of the stable door in the kitchen to greet Auntie Ann. Despite this foolhardiness she made a full recovery and has never been ill in her life, the only problem being that she will sometimes bring a limp on herself by overexertion. She does not take kindly to enforced rest, so that even after being spayed she was soon back in action. We would have loved her to have puppies, and feel sure she would have been a good mother, but there are too many dogs already needing homes to bring any more mix-ups into the world. The vet was very supportive and assured us that most bitches benefit from being spayed, avoiding the gynae problems which often occur in later life for those who have not had the operation.

****

I admire people who puppy walk for Guide Dogs for the Blind, for while house-training is not overly difficult with a responsive pup, it's a relief when it's safely achieved. I wouldn't have wanted to start all over again in a few months time. Rosie rapidly got the message and was quite 'safe' to take visiting to Broadstairs, where Graham's brother, wife and family live. It was the first time we had taken her away to stay and we were very proud of her; she was the per-fect guest, being very polite to their Siamese cat. On the last morning we took her for a good run on the beach, which she found enthralling, splashing into the swooshing pond of the sea was high adventure and totally absorbing. So much so that she forgot other more mundane matters. As we approached London in the car she began a piteous whining. We could guess what the problem might be, but stopping was impossible. We drove on, the whining grew more intense, till at last, about twenty or thirty minutes later we were able to pull in and offer her a suitable grassy spot. She rushed off, her level of relief only matched by the length of the squat, which was worthy of a tenancy. We could not help laughing but she cast us a reproachful look which said, "It's all right for you lot!" She has, in fact, grown up with a tank like a camel. In the win-ter it is nothing for her to have her last 'out' about four o'clock, flatly refusing to consider the garden either at bedtime or early morning. She will wait unperturbed till we are ready for her proper walk, which though usually early, may be delayed till ten o'clock at weekends.

****

Rosie, like Timma, took a lot of persuading that leads were ever necessary on walks. I had tried to get her used to the lead in the garden and she seemed to think it was quite fun, but then when we began proper walks up the field and the hill, she decided that free range was what it was all about and that leads were only for babies. The trouble was, that whereas most of the time in the areas we walk a lead is unnecessary, on occasion they are essential. This was a hard message to get across. There was at least one embarrassing walk with my friend Carole (another of Rosie's favourite people) when I needed to put her on the lead, and she stood there, defiantly barking and keeping just out of range. As soon as we continued walking and throwing her stick she shut up again. Fortunately the road was a quiet one through the forest and we managed, but it was very unsatisfactory.

I was not sure what to do about it, but more by luck than judgement, let well alone for a month or two, only going on walks where I knew she would not need the lead. Then one day I took her along the canal bank to the bridge which carries the main road traffic. As I started moving up the path towards the road where she could see and hear the rumbling, I simply said, "Oh Rosie, there's the ROAD." She came immediately to have her lead put on, and we have never had a moment's trouble since. She seems to accept that the lead is for her own protection and feels safe on it.

****

If life were fair and dogs were predictable with no minds of their own, then ours would be unswervingly loyal to me, who, after all, put in all the basic mothering and caring when she was young, and spends the most time with her now she is grown. Rosie has set ideas of her own however, and while it is always to me she runs to have minor hurts rubbed better, I do not get a look in when Graham is around. She immediately becomes "Daddy's girl" wanting to sit on his knee (which is a mixed blessing, as she's much too large to be a lapdog) and demanding that he walk her, regardless of any efforts I might have already made when he is pushed for time. She succeeds in bullying him almost as much as Timma did. Rosie will not tolerate any kind of shouting, making a reproachful retreat to a handy barn, disregarding the fact that the raised voice is in no way directed at her but merely the result of a tough day at the office!

On balance, she probably prefers men to women, and another of her favourite people was Gordon, the gardener who replaced Mr Jenkins when he finally had to admit, "I've not got enough puff." (We have kept in touch and he has made approving remarks of what has happened to his jungle in subsequent years.) Gordon was a plant of a very different foliage. Whereas Mr Jenkins could hardly be persuaded across the threshold, Gordon was instantly eager to come in for a chat with his tea and never in much of a hurry to leave the kitchen and get back to the gardening. He was good once he got his hands into the earth, but even better at playing with Rosie, who came to regard his visits as entirely for her benefit. Gordon on the other hand came to think of us as a good place to watch television, especially if the only cats around were the four-legged kind, being looked after by the mice of Harry and Hugo. We would get back from a London weekend to find a merry huddle round the telly!

There was one occasion though, when I was trying to cook a meal and watch an absorbing Wimbledon match through the hatchway at the same time. This kind of double activity is never easy, but I wondered why I was finding it so nearly impossible, until it registered that I was endeavouring to peer over Gordon's shoulder as he leaned ever more enthusiastically into the open hatch to get closer to the action.

To be fair, the garden came to no great harm under Gordon's spasmodic care, though it could have done when he took down the old and rotting ranch fencing before he was sure of delivery of the new green wire mesh. The idea was to install a strong but invisible device to keep the cows on their side of the well-developed hedge. The day had its ironies. Gordon's timing was perfect as it coincided with the cows first ecstatic cavortings into the field after being indoors all winter; a time when the meadow grass may be sweet but not half so tempting as beech hedge and the luscious shrubs on our side of the divide. It was only after the old fencing was down that it became clear the new would not be arriving until the next day, by which time the cows would have clog-danced the lawn to pulp and Gordon's mate would no longer be available to help him, which was a shame, as the mate might have been able to tell the posts from the wire. We were able to persuade the obliging farmer to relocate his cows for forty-eight hours, and to encourage Harry to act as Gordon's mate when the chain link fence finally arrived, but the resulting wobble of green wire has remained a feature which we unsportingly pretend was inherited from posterity; for it was never totally clear who knew less about creating a decent fence, Harry or Gordon, but we suspect it was the latter.

****

Gordon stayed with us through one summer, but unlike the swallow did not return with the next. He probably felt that we were not supplying him with a proper quotient of televiewing time and moved on to more amenable sur-roundings, leaving us in our relief to find gardening help more suited to our needs.

Chapter Twenty Five

Slugging and Searching

I deferred to Rosie's best friend Carole for advice on finding the right help in the garden, as she has various horticultural qualifications, not least among them the planting of a veritable forest on the high hill of her home. She had been helped in this project by Simon, a young contract gardener with whom she had been impressed.

She was happy to recommend him, and it soon became clear why. The grim stories I had heard in the past about employing contract gardeners could not apply, for not only was Simon the head of the firm, he and two other young men *were* the firm. There could be no danger of people loose in the garden who might sever the artery of a prized *Clematis montana*, or mistake carefully nurtured honesty seedlings for weeds. The only snag in the system proved to be the obvious one, that the team only came to us once a fortnight.

They put in their intensive hours no matter what, working in wellies and water-proofs through the sourest winter weather and this devotion to duty is usually enough, but there are patches in the growing months when there is so much happening almost on a daily basis that it would be good to have a few more hours dotted among the block bookings, particularly when I was experiencing the back trouble which frustrated my gardening in recent years.

On the whole though, the system works well, better than I could ever have thought, Simon is not only knowledgeable but is sympathetic to plants being left to be themselves as far as possible. He and I seldom disagree, though we did once have a semi-serious misunderstanding. The horrid holly had escaped from its neat green ball and was making menacing movements in the direction of the kitchen, so I asked Simon to prune it hard back. I then went out - a silly habit - and returned to find he had taken me at my word. There, swathed in a thigh hugging flow of glossy green periwinkle skirt starred with blue flowers, was a curvaceous stump with two arms; as mutilated as that famous statue which I admire, but find hard to love. We had 'Venus de Milo' in the garden for many months before threatenings from me to turn her into a bird table and pos-sible secret pleadings from Simon to "show a leaf," produced a few tentative sprouts heralding recovery.

****

The pink weeping cherry tree in the middle of the small front lawn was not so lucky. Whether it was old age or merely being overshadowed by so many larger trees we did not know, but it had started to look poorly before Simon joined us, and soon after his arrival we had to pronounce it dead. It was a pretty little tree and I was sad to see it go, but we agreed it was too tough a location for any new plant to try to become established. I therefore decided to replace it with a planned statue.

You have to be careful with statues or they can look either pretentious or twee, though like choosing a picture for the house it is a very personal matter, and I have sneaking sympathy with people who turn their gardens into gnome sanctuaries. After all, these colourful characters give pleasure to their owners and their cheerful harmlessness can at worst offend 'good taste' which is rather less damaging than the toxic sprays and slug pellets used by some people who profess concern for natural beauty in the garden.

However, I did not think that gnomes were the answer for us, I wanted something in plain stone that would be in keeping with the mood of subtle magic we had managed to sustain in the front garden. The statue would have light spilled on it from the Narnia Lamp, so it was important that it should look well by night as well as day.

It was one of those situations where I did not quite know what I wanted but would recognise it the moment I found it, which reminds me of something that was apparently once said about my grandmother in the stormy middle years of her marriage: "The trouble with Doff is that she doesn't know what she wants, but she damn well means to have it!"

Well, I found it - her - among antique garden ornaments near Little Venice in London. She was a beautiful stone lady (with arms) gracefuly draped and carrying a pitcher. She was perfect and could have been ours for a mere £7,000!

Even garden ornaments without legs have been known to walk from front gardens, so anything mildly expensive was not in our sights, let alone that sort of price, but at least she had given me a little more idea of what I was seeking; something with some movement in the moulding. In a local garden centre I eventually found exactly what I had not known I was looking for . . . 'Romeo and Juliet' at £38.50p.

They were an instant and continuing success; less than two feet in height they are secure in their love through day, night, and all seasons of the year, clasped to each other cloaked in snow, or looking as if they could suddenly dance through the yellow poppies that shoulder them in early summer, and then tread carefully so as not to crush the begonias that dedazzle their feet from July.

****

I used not to like begonias. I found them rather uninteresting, but poor relationships with most other bedding plants has taught me otherwise: all that blossoms will not bloom, at least not here it won't. Pansies, lobelias, petunias, nemesias... you name them, they won't. But begonias do not mind if they get no sun and all rain, they do not mind if it is sunny and you do not water them for a few days, they are incurably optimistic, good-natured and reliable. Best of all, they lack slug appeal.

How sad to be a slug. The kindest of people, even those who assiduously find suitable alternative accommodation for their house spiders in the garage or garden shed, think nothing of murdering slugs. There is no sympathy spared, people will sprinkle salt on them and watch them disintegrate in slimy agony. Organically minded people now set parasitic worms on them (nematodes) which does not seem very sporting, surely trapping them in pots of beer is much kinder. No method seems to be fully effective and since birds do not find slugs a dainty dish the best organic method of control is probably to advertise for a family of hedgehogs. At the end of July we usually have to suspend lawn mowing for a week or more as thousands of minuscule baby frogs make pilgrimage across our garden from the reservoirs to the big beyond. Perhaps I should make more effort to persuade them to stay, or put up posters to encourage them to return when they are old enough to come on the job market, for we seldom see adult frogs in the garden, and as yet I have not been contacted by any hedgehog representative. There is a toad patrol but it is only partially successful, maybe due to under staffing, so I have been known to resort to a powder which is guaranteed harmless to everything but slugs (though it also disappears into the ground at the first sign of rain) and to protecting plants by putting sand or cat litter round their roots as slugs hate crawling over anything abrasive. I will not use slug pellets as I am far from convinced that they are harmless to wildlife, and one theory for the decline of the song thrush pinpoints the pellet. Besides, I do not wish the slugs any harm, merely that they could have the same sort of regard for my plants.

Maureen used to rescue honeybees frantic against an unyielding window by rafting them to safety on a flower, for in this way they would not feel threatened, use their sting and as a consequence die a painful death. Even she was not fond of slugs but recognised their right to be. Her solution was to trap them under grapefruit, then gather up the marauders in a bucket and take them to the woods to feast themselves there, but I doubt if even this kindly method was all conquering. Hence, I follow the path of the possible and limit the menu to plants that might send the slugs searching for more promising catering arrangements. Begonias are top of my list, but Simon also recommends verbena and bedding geraniums. There may well be others. Seek them out.

****

Just before the final demise of the weeping cherry tree there was another loss to bear. Nelle had never had very robust health, and it became clear towards Christmas that she was seriously unwell. I began to prepare myself for the inevitable, and made sure she enjoyed the season with the best of the titbits. It was a graceful decline, made easier because I had felt she had been on extended loan to us for quite some while, so that every month she was still with us was a bonus.

One of her favourite places to sit (and she had several) was on the ghetto blaster on the wide worktop in the kitchen. The machine was affectionately known as the 'Woofah', and Nelle would settle herself comfortably, feet tucked under, to listen to her favourite music and radio programmes. During her last few days with us, she was joined several times by all three of the other cats, sitting round her in a protective clowder* as if they sensed that she was fading. It was touching and a help to me, for they were confirming what I knew I would soon have to do. Nelle never minded going to the vet and she slipped from us quietly, her time fulfilled, but I can still see that pink rosebud of a nose.

****

It was February. I did not want to rush into replacing her. She, after all, had found us, and I felt I would like to wait for another cat to materialise when it was ready. Nothing happened for several months, then in September I received a flattering phone call:

"I have got these beautiful half Abyssinian kittens, and I've been told that you might be a suitable home."

*collective noun for cats

138

Chapter Twenty Six

The Hooker

It transpired that a mutual friend, knowing we were one cat short, had recommended me, and the next day I went to be interviewed, having told Barbara during our telephone conversation that we would be looking for a female kitten to restore balance to the household. There were three kittens in the litter, one male and two females of which one was already booked. Barbara had several adult Abyssinian cats, all with imaginative names, and our intended was known as 'Violet Elizabeth' as she was unusually determined to have her own way.

I could see why Barbara was fussy about the credentials of anyone lucky enough to be awarded one of her kittens. Her husband was an architect and the large two hundred year old house was designed as a cats' palace, with every possible feline amenity of the sensible kind; there was a blanket along the back of the aga, and a wonderful high shelf with a cosy box on top, where cats could climb and sleep or view the activity on the plain below. There were plenty of toys for the kittens, and ready cat flap access to the large walled garden with its fascination of trees and pond-watching for the older cats. Although keen to produce good pedigree Abysssinian kittens, Barbara liked her cats to live as full a feline life as possible, thus Grishkin, the mother of this litter, had twitched her independent whiskers and chosen her own partner, thank you very much - a large black and white moggy.

As I sat there being investigated by the full team and growing rapidly to appreciate the special qualities of Abyssinians, their sleek coats of burnt orange and their affectionate disposition, it became apparent that Violet Elizabeth had made up her mind. If her mother had chosen who was to be the father of her kittens, so Violet Elizabeth was going to have a say in choosing who "might do" as a prospective adoptive mum. It was not me, whom she found unutterably boring compared with the game of batting a ball of silver foil around the floor.

This would have been depressing but for the temporarily named "Tom Kitten" who also needed a home. His mind was made up as swiftly and decisively as his sister's; I would certainly do. He purred, he nestled, he played with the pendant round my neck. Barbara and I were defeated. I had been chosen. This little blue-eyed boy wanted to come and live with us. There could be no argument. It would tip the balance at home to three males and only one female, but I was confident that Daisy May had the personality to cope.

The kittens were almost ready to leave their mother, but we were going to India for ten days in early October, so it was agreed that we would collect the new baby on our return, by which time we would, of course, have thought of his permanent name; something suitable, something exotic and oriental.

****

Our trip to India was too short. We fell in love with this land of diamonds and dust. We wondered and gasped at the intermingled beauty and poverty of the places we visited, and learnt just enough to know that there are no easy answers to her many contradictions, and certainly none that we would have the presumption to offer. We did however absorb the resonance of names and came home with the decision made; as a memento of our journey to Agra and the Taj Mahal our kitten would be called 'Taj'.

Neither of our sons has inherited a passion for cats, so that news of a kitten was treated by them with nonchalance. In any case Harry was away studying. Hugo, however, greeted the arrival of the cat basket with typical teenage unenthusiasm as he raised his eyes from the television to say, "Oh well, let's have a look at this kitten then."

I opened the basket and two huge ears peeped up at us followed by eyes and whiskers. Hugo's laconicism disintegrated into a soppy grin as he affectionately pronounced, "You *CAN'T* call him *'TAJ'*. He's 'Bernard'," and promptly took the kitten over. So much for intensively planning the name of your pet.

****

It was a joy to have a kitten. Bernard was adorable and fun. His ears predominated his person for some weeks till he grew into them, and we have photos of him wearing Paddington Bear's hat (a relic of Hugo's childhood) in which skilfully placed holes were cut to accommodate Bernard's ears. He was happy to sport this headdress for short periods, and spent hours in Hugo's room, being amused with toys or cuddled up asleep.

Bernard's introduction to the other animals was not a problem, though we took some care that there were no surprise confrontations. Rosie merely wagged her tail mildly, and after one initial spit in her direction Bernard decided she was huge and warm and cuddly and an indispensable part of his lifestyle. She in her turn happily accepted him, so long as she could rest her nose in the lap that he was sitting in.

His relationships with the other cats was rather more complex. Moses welcomed him with his usual easy acceptance of any newcomer, and Silvester was visibly pleased to have someone else to play with, but there was never any possibility of the Moses-Silvester axis of friendship being damaged. They were bonded, forever close.

Daisy May continued her affectionate if slightly distant relationship with Moses and her sparky one with Silvester whom she continued to pretend to hate, hurling venomous abuse at him one minute, only to be found curled up beside him on our bed a few minutes later. She accepted Bernard's arrival in the sense that she never threatened to leave home. She did not leave notes about the place saying "It's him or me," but she never really grew to like him. When he was small, his inevitable teasing, coming from the junior irk she found beyond the pale, and she would tick him off and then stalk off with the dignity of an affronted prima donna. Now he is grown up, he tends to delegate the teasing to Silvester, who is more than competent at it, but Daisy will spit at Bernard as soon as look at him. He deals with this by affably ignoring her bad grace, but maybe for her sake I should have followed the original plan and had another female - Daisy May and Violent Elizabeth (as she came to be called) might have got along famously!

Cats are territorial creatures and with Bernard's arrival a problem entered the house - spraying. Moses and Silvester, though both fond of him began scent marking indoors. Fortunately, Moses being so much older, made his point for a week or two and then rested on his venerable laurels. Silvester however, has continued to need to stake his claim. Hormone tablets have not helped much, so it's out with the lavender water to counter the effects. It's also out with Silvester as frequently as I can manage, though he treats these affronts on his person with undiminished good humour. Put out the front door at 07.00 hours, the cat flap at the kitchen end of the house can be heard flapping at 07.00 and 29 seconds as he makes his cheery re-entry looking for breakfast. Despite the problem, Silvester remains a tonic; a lesson to all of us in how not to be downhearted.

****

Bernard grew as kittens do. He grew into his ears, grew great yellow lamps in place of small blue ones and a tail that wafted long and slender. His feet remained small, but then anybody's would look neat and sweet compared with those of Bigfoot. Whereas a pure bred Abyssinian has only a small white bib under the chin, Bernard has a white T-shirt and three-and-a-bit white paws. The rest of his coat is an oriental silken rug, an interweave of grey and black reminiscent of a rabbit, his legs have delicate tiger bars of black, while his lower tummy has longer and lusher fur in apricot orange.

He was enthralled by the preparations for Christmas, diving in ecstatic rustles under the wrapping paper, swinging on string and patting the balls off the Christmas tree almost as fast as I could put them on. The cats have always loved Christmas, it is the one time of year when they are allowed to come into the 'best' room. They are normally barred from its velour of curtains and furniture, and anywhere banned is, of course, immediately more desirable, especially if, when you do achieve entry it is full of cats' favourite textures and surfaces. Then there is the arrival of the turkey. This causes great interest in its raw state, and the smell of the giblets cooking creates anticipatory pacing and wrinkling of noses. When the bird comes out of the oven there is always much proffered help with taking the meat from the bones. But all this anticipation and threats of robbery turn cool along with the giblets when the cats are *given* some leftovers. Food loses its piquancy once it becomes legitimate.

Bernard's first Christmas Day was something of a disaster for him, and nearly one for us, for which I take the blame. My parents' current dog who had then been with them about eighteen months (having been rehomed from our local animal sanctuary) is allegedly the same crossbreed as Rosie but the nearest you could call him to a Labradollie is a lad. Not that there is an ounce of malice in him, he adores everybody but shows it by overexuberance, particularly when visiting our house. This soon wears off and then he settles down and is perfectly well behaved, so I'd airily said, "Oh don't worry just let him roar about till he's got it out of his system."

It was the first time Bruno had been round to us since Bernard's arrival. I should have remembered and effected a proper introduction. I should also have remembered that Bernard was asleep on our bed. There was a sudden terrified rumpus as Bernard bulleted down the stairs, through the dining room, across the Christmas table, laden with silver and best glasses, and flew up the curtains urinating on the window in his panic.

My mother grabbed Bruno, I clutched and comforted Bernard as best I could, till he broke from me and escaped to the safety of outdoors, where he resolutely stayed till Bruno had left the premises in the evening. Miraculously, the table had escaped damage, and we have never had to worry since then about cats in the carving at Christmas, Bruno's reputation has seen to that, but harm was done because Bernard has remained terrified of Bruno ever since, and worse still he is suspiciously afraid of any visiting dog, no matter how well-mannered. Forunately, Rosie is in a class of her own, maybe considered to be an honorary cat. Bernard rubs round and under her as devotedly as Moses, who for all his great age is the least bothered by visiting dogs, always giving them the benefit of the doubt.

****

One of Bernard's characteristics is his relative nervousness; "nervous as a kitten" could have been coined for him, though it is probably more true of him in maturity than when he was tiny. Any sharp sound or swift movement, even from someone he knows well, can send him scurrying, even when he is in the middle of a meal. On the other hand, he is an intrepid defender of his territory against other cats, and a keen hunter. He is well camouflaged for the pursuit, and being young leads the fullest feline life in the household. He is usually out at night, returning late for breakfast and then picking a comfortable chair on which to snooze for a few hours before going on the day shift. More than once we have found behind the television or the settee, the remains of a corpse consisting of little more than the tail of his squirrel victim. Squirrels are not easy customers to tackle, and on two occasions he has suffered an abscess, either from that kind of encounter or from an entanglement with another cat in the area.

One Sunday morning over breakfast we were privileged to watch a comic confrontation between Bernard and a magpie, both of whom were perched in the cherry tree at the end of the garden. The bird was obviously enjoying teasing him, muttering insults from a safe distance, and then, as Bernard began to edge closer along the branch, hopping to a new perch just out of reach above his irritated head, to continue the cheeky chatter. At last, Bernard was provoked into making a savage but unsuitable lunge which caused him to fall out of the tree onto the grass, while the magpie, killing itself laughing, flew to the top of the tree to gloat at being king of its castle.

Bernard was far from amused, and we were glad to be safely hidden indoors, lest he should hear our giggling. He would have been very offended, for of course you should never ever laugh *at* a cat, only *with* a cat who is deliberately playing the fool to entertain you. Bernard was not trying to be funny, he had just suffered the indignity of being bettered by a bird. I knew what was coming; he followed to the letter that famous maxim from Paul Gallico's 'Jennie', "When in doubt, wash." He sat in the sun soothing his ego with rhythmic licking, pretending that he had merely grown bored by the stupid magpie and had leapt down athletically and purposefully to attend to more prestigious affairs.

****

Bernard will allow a cuddle for the briefest of moments, but he does not really like to be picked up - few cats do - though he is enthusiastically affectionate on his own terms when the mood takes him. You can therefore imagine that visits to the vet are anathema to him. He hated going for his injections and as for going to be neutered ... what he thought about that would be unprintable, for the degradation of being trapped in a cat basket and hoicked to the vet even when ill, is to Bernard, the nadir of any feline programme.

There was one tea time, when he had come in for his meal with one side of his face puffed up like a cannon ball. He allowed me to bathe it and some very nasty gunge was released, so I took him down to evening surgery. Poor Bernard, not only did he resent this excursion when he was feeling under the weather anyway, but he was as always, very frightened, quivering to a tremble as the vet examined him. On this occasion, a quick shot of antibiotic and advice about continuing the bathing should not have been too upsetting, but Bernard exploded from the basket and off into the garden to check out a favourite tree the moment we touched down on home soil.

That night, Graham being away, I was as alone in the marital bed as it is possible to be with a dog who not only snuggles up, but eases me towards the last third of the mattress while at least two cats covert the warmth of my leg-space. I suppose I feel safe, thus surrounded, for I always manage to sleep very soundly. On this particular night I was awoken in the small hours by a gentle rasping lick on my cheek. It was Bernard come to say, "Thanks mum, I don't half feel better."

Because he is wilder, more nervous than the others, his demonstrations of affection are all the more moving, and although he rarely sleeps on the bed with us, he is the only one of the cats ever to meander right under the bed-clothes and snuggle close, as he did one Siberian winter's night. He crept against me in the deep-frozen hours with rapturous purring, his coat as smooth as ice cream and as cold.

We are used to being pounded and purred upon by Silvester and Daisy May, we take it for granted along with the gentler attentions of Moses, but when Bernard arrives in your lap it is a rare honour and you are foolish not to savour it. In these moments I will not be stirred, short of the house catching fire. There is nothing more soothing than the purr of a contented cat on your knee, but the pleasure is heightened when the gift is bestowed rarely, like a prize.

We have never had another cat as keen on gardening as Sam, but most have taken a mild interest. Bernard's main fascination comes during the winter

Haiku (on being picked up)

Don't. It's a favour
bestowed only when earned, for
I am my own self.

months when all the potted plants are in the garden room and ritual watering takes place. He likes to help — testing the water temperature by hooking his paw through the fall of water onto each plant and giving me the nod to move onto the next recipient.

I could pick one characteristic to typify each of our cats, and if I were to do it for Bernard it would be his habit of reaching out with his paw, especially from the major worktop in the kitchen as you walk by him. With his delicately striped leg, his claws not out, but hinting at their metal, he makes a hooking movement into any passing bit of you he can grab, informing you that it is high time for you to give him priority attention, whether it is his main meal or some elevensies; a snack which he could decide to take as ninesies, tensies or twelvesies.

With charm, cheek and courtesy, he makes his requirements clear. Bernard the hooker.

Chapter Twenty Seven

Too Many Magpies — Not Enough Thrushes

There have been changes along the lane during the years that we have lived here, of course there have. Change in some measure is as inevitable as birthdays, and although we may not like it, any more than we relish the prospect of growing old, there is only one alternative, and most of us are not yet ready for that.

We have been lucky in our tucked away area, for it has been much less affected than the main town, which has grown massively, had an inaptly named 'ring road' put through the middle of it, and seen the demise of many of the small shops which gave it so much character. Our neighbourhood is protected by conservation laws, so that although the number of dwellings has increased from five to eight, this has only occurred by dint of turning existing elderly buildings, such as stables, into houses. It would be unreasonable to object to this, especially when we have such good neighbours, sharing a sense of community that so much of Britain has lost.

It is inevitable too, that over a period not far off twenty years there have been changes in the household. Our sons are grown, and we naturally see less of them. Animals mature, and in growing older sometimes have health problems. It is as important for us to have faith in our vet as it is in our family doctor.

****

In the months before Bernard's arrival, we had some concern about Daisy May who was having trouble in keeping her food down. The vet could find nothing obviously wrong with her, but suggested moving her onto a prescriptive diet formulated to guard against cats' vulnerability to kidney disease. It consists of dried biscuits, but these should not be confused with 'bickies' those tempting tasties with which most of us supplement our cats' food, and which are too high in protein to be either resistible or good for your cat if given in any quantity.

The vet's biscuits looked boring to me, but Daisy May took to them well, too well, as she rapidly put on weight, losing her slender shape to become more rounded and matronly. Moses and Silvester showed no interest in this newfangled dietary food, and continued with their usual feline menu of tinned food and 'bickies', which I also gave Bernard on his arrival. To my astonishment, once he discovered Daisy's C/D diet he announced that that was what he would like in future please, and proceeded to turn his nose up at any other arrangements.

That left Moses and Silvester still eating to the old routine, but after another year or so, Silvester, who had always been the rangy one, began to show the telltale sign of sinking-in around the haunches. I was fearful that kidney trouble was starting and not surprisingly the vet's advice was to move him firmly onto the C/D diet even though he had never shown any interest in it. It would not have been practical to try to allow Moses to keep to a separate menu, and the change would probably be good for him anyway, so out went the tinned food, out went the 'bickies', and in came a huge packet of vet's biscuits. There was no choice available.

Moses almost immediately accepted the situation and began tucking in, but Silvester was not impressed. For two days he sniffed around the dried-up pellets looking at me and chirruping with good-natured disbelief, making me feel brutal, though I was not concerned that he would come to any harm if he did not eat for a day or three. There are tales of cats surviving for two weeks or more trapped under floorboards with no water, never mind food, and of course the advice was, "He'll eat when he's hungry." He did. At first with no great relish but gradually finding the pellets more palatable, he soon adjusted to his healthier diet. The benefits were swift to manifest, within weeks he began to fill out in the right places and his coat took on a sheen it had never shown before.

Silvester will never be fat, it is not in his inheritance, for I suppose that cats, like people have varying metabolisms, and some as they grow older have a tendency to put on weight. Daisy May went through a worrying phase for a year or more, when she looked, not just plump but pregnant, and her sides were sensitive to the touch. I suspected something sinister, but regular veterinary checks revealed nothing, and apart from being sick if she ate more than small amounts at a time and being rather more irrascible than usual she appeared healthy enough. It seemed pointless to subject her to complex and uncomfortable tests just to satisfy curiosity about the underlying cause. Following the vet's advice, for a long time I put a drop of a prescribed medicine on her food as this seemed to help with the nausea, but then we evolved a feeding pattern: ten biscuits, pause, ten biscuits, pause, ten biscuits, pause, until she had had about half of what the other cats would eat. This ad hoc treatment for her unknown digestive problem appeared to achieve results, or else it miraculously righted itself, for suddenly Daisy May lost her pregnant balloon look and has settled into being comfortably plump with a glossier coat and a sweeter nature again.

****

In the garden, we have noted, as most people have, the increase in magpie numbers and the sad decline of the song thrush, but other small birds such as the pied wagtail seem to be thriving, though this summer we have been concerned about our 'mad' wagtail who has spent six solid weeks during daylight hours fluttering against, and dropping droppings upon, several of our windows, trying to frighten away the rival, who, in his anxious wagtail mind lives in or beyond the glass. I was worried that he would wear himself out with such fruitless effort. Initially, I used *The Financial Times* as a wagtail deterrent all over the first offending area, which was our bedroom patio doors. We were left groping around in a room with the light level of a grotto, but the wagtail then decided that his rival had sneakily moved off and was mounting a challenge from a downstairs window instead. I did not think we had enough copies of the 'FT' to cover the entire glass mass of the house, so I drew curtains here and there with limited effect, until at last he decided the battle was won, or lost, and he gave up the struggle, but I fear he should have been making better use of his time.

****

The daphne that I planted for Nelle, alas, has not flourished, but I have just discovered an enchanting little rose called 'Bo-peep', which I am going to plant in its place. It is covered in small pink frilly blooms and tiny buds, every bit as delicate and pretty as Nelle's nose. If it takes it will be the perfect reminder.

The winter cherry trees continue to brighten the darker months of the year, though they have never bloomed so early nor in such profusion as they did to greet us the November of our arrival. They, like many other trees in the garden have grown very big and it will soon be time to take a serious look at which branches need to come off, and to consider whether any tree needs to be removed to give its neighbour space to grow. Conversely, having taken a long time to find a possible solution to the ugliness of the house wall that rises behind the balcony, the virginia creeper on whom we are pinning our hopes is progessing but slowly, despite pleading encouragement. Recognising that it is a chilly corner for a young creep to start exploring, this winter we plan to cosset it in a thermal vest. These can now be purchased at local garden centres, and come on the roll, so that you can tailor-make the vest to the style of your plant.

It is wonderfully satisfying when plants do well, but then problems can arise because a plant is too invasive, encroaching on its compatriots. I have recently found that I have been careless enough to allow a kerria to push a spirea almost out of bed, and a large white rhododendron to mug a small red one, spreading its smothering glossiness to intimidate the latter into losing half its leaves. Bullying happens in the garden unless you keep a constant watchful eye.

Perhaps plants are territorial like cats. A year or so after Bernard arrived, the family who live in the converted stables across the lane to us, acquired a kitten. George is a 'Jellicle', black and white and smooth and neat. He would like to include our garden on his beat, and Rosie would have no objection as she and George enjoy a mutual respect, but our cats, especially Bernard, will not tolerate the idea, and there have been a few arguments, eventually resolved in a negotiated settlement; our driveway is considered neutral ground, and the bonnets of our cars are George's prerogative. He enjoys them most when they are warm from a journey, but it is not unusual to start the day reversing with an unruffled cat sitting comfortably over the engine. It is only as you ease the car forwards and onwards into the lane that George with a nonchalant shrug jumps down to safety and strolls casually away, convinced that he has done you a favour by gracing your vehicle with his presence, even being kind enough to leave the signature of his paw marks as a memento.

****

The only structural work of note that we have made to the house recently was the addition of a garden room or conservatory about four years ago. Because the born-again balcony had a solid floor and thus formed half the roof for this new living space, it made sense for the remaining section of roof to be tiled rather than made of glass. This has proved to be a boon, for the room would have been unbearably hot otherwise. As it is, it makes a pleasant addition to the living room, is perfect for overwintering plants, and comes into its own for parties and at Christmas, when the coloured lights reflect and reflect and reflect....

The real reason for the garden room however, took a while to unfold, and only became clear as a result of some unpleasant leaking, which made the ceiling look as if we were making experiments in mould growing. We did not rate this greeny-blue creeping fungus as a desirable feature, so asked our builders to try to remove its underlying cause. They are not easily defeated and we have great faith in them, but it took a while to track the problem to our much loved wooden balustrade which, exposed to the ferocity of weather, had wilted enough for water to sneak into its base and then to seep surreptitiously into the ceiling below.

It was sad to see the wooden rail disappear, and its first metal replacement was an expensive mistake, chosen too quickly. I hated it the moment it arrived. It was well made and would have looked fine on a more modern house, but on ours its curvaceous sides bulged like a skeletal ribcage. I painted it green to try to soften it, I tried looking at it from all angles, trying to find one from where I might begin to like and then love it. It was no good, I had boobed and it had to go, in favour of an elegant older design, cast at a specialist firm in the town. This time I was well-satisfied with the result, but more importantly there was enough space between these beautiful flowered railings for cats to wend their way onto what Daisy May and Moses soon decided was a sunroof designed in their honour. They sit companionably out there by the hour in the fine weather, so much so that the vet advised sun block for Daisy's vulnerable pale ears.

Some people might consider it an extravagance to have constructed a garden room, balcony and balustrade in order to make the perfect sunbathing space for Daisy May and Moses, but we have no regrets. Cynics will say that a cat stays anywhere that there is enough food, but I think there is far more to creating contentment for a cat. I still get a pleasurable tingle when I consider that free as they are to go anywhere they please to live, they choose to stay here with us. Maybe we are doing something right.

Chapter Twenty Eight

"When the moon is wide ..."

Moses has now turned seventeen. His character has changed, mellowing with age into a cuddly old softy who hardly bothers to go out. He makes camp in our bedroom, either on or under the bed, though sometimes for a change he disappears into the dark cave of the airing cupboard, or takes to his designer sunroof on warm days.

As cats grow older their claws become much less retractible, and about a year ago he injured his own eye, which meant visits to the vet and me squeezing ointment into the sore area several times a day. This seemed to bring us much closer together, and he decided that maybe after sixteen years I was someone worthy of his trust and affection.

Moses has small opportunity now to wear down his claws on the lilac tree, and they were growing so long that they were snagging in my clothing. One night a claw became so entangled in the bedspread that the only option was to cut a hole in it to free him. After that, I enquired about having his claws trimmed and it proved both easy and painless, especially when he found it was the locum vet. For her, any patient I have taken, becomes instantly limp and co-operative with adoration.

I had been afraid that the claw cutting might mean a general anaesthetic, which had been administered only a few weeks before to sort out Moses' elderly, ailing teeth. Poor old chap, it left him mightily groggy; he hardly came out from under our bed for three days. I had to provide a tray in the bathroom, and a mashed fish convalescent diet.

The reward came a few days later when I was working in the bedroom, and tossed some screwed up rough paper onto the floor by my chair. A rejuvenated kitten began batting it around the carpet and has been in high good humour ever since. He had probably been suffering from low grade toothache for a while, and we all know the burst of energy that comes with release from pain. Every so often he assures me of his devotion by nibbling my bare toes as I pad across the bedroom and stop to talk to him, or he will attack them on a hot night if I am sitting up reading on top of the covers. It's quite painful in a ticklish sort of way but the intention is so good it's not possible to mind.

****

Moses appears to stay close to base, but even in old age cats may have their secrets. Two years ago we met some people at a friend's house, and the conversation turned to pets. They said how worried they were about this poor old cat who wandered into their garden through the back hedge every morning, to sit pathetically miaouing until they went out and fed him; several times. He still looked half starved and ill-treated. He would come into the house sometimes and sit on a best chair if the weather was bad, but always disappeared again about six o'clock. I thought I recognised this 'Artful Dodger', and when I checked on the location, sure enough it was Big Ern, aged twenty-two, who had belonged to my friend Maureen, along with Daisy May. I still visited her mother regularly, who adored the remaining cats, had told me several times that she worried where Ernie went all day, and that sometimes he would be late home for his supper, though when he did appear he ate with gusto.

For our part we are lucky to know tolerant people with a sense of humour, who do not come complaining about being woken in the night, for Silvester and Bernard are cat burglars, and not very quiet ones at that. Mercedes and Parsley who live next door to us, wear collars with devices that are programmed to open their personalised cat flap. This prevents unauthorised personnel from entering the building. That is the theory. In practice, my two thugs take a running jump at the petrified plastic and bludgeon it into submission. Having broken and entered they then proceed at a leisurely pace to see what delicious fishy pickings have been left on their victims' plates.

I think I know my cats well, but I had no idea, of course, that two of them were up to such skulduggery. T. S. Eliot suggested that cats operate under more than one name, that they are merely obliging us by responding to 'Sam' or 'Bernard', whereas they know themselves by other more mystic names; an appealing thought. I love my cats and they love me, but they are only 'mine' in so far as they choose to be. If your cat has the sort of freedom that I believe cats should enjoy as their right, then there can be no way of knowing all their movements, let alone what goes on inside their mysterious heads. "What dreams may come...?" even to dear old Moses in his camp under our bed.

****

There is a small stable near the corner of our lane, with ample green space for two horses, a donkey and two or three cats. The fields slope up and into the hill, our hill, where the moon rises.

Last spring, arriving home in the early evening, I glanced into the field as I drove round the corner, and had to stop the car to check that I was not imagining what I thought I had seen. The white horse, caught in the last rays of sun, was walking gently up the sloping grass, while riding bareback, where the saddle would have been, was a black cat, with its feet tucked under, comfy as a tea cosy, surveying both the scenery and the horse's supple flow of tail.

This unlikely but enchanting picture set me wondering. If you include the stables, there are at least eighteen cats who live in our immediate neighbourhood, and there are more horses higher up the hill. Could there be a nocturnal meeting of free spirits; horses and cats exploring together as the night settles and stars pinprick the dark?

May cats always keep wildness and mystery as part of their being. Who knows whether there are times, when they do not merely dance into trees or quirk across lawns, but gather to gallop on favourite steeds, high and deep into a secret sky?

POEMS

Remembrance *for Sam*

The shadow of your purr
stirs the leaves.

Memories move through the garden,
soft as fur.

Though other well-loved paws
will pad and claw the earth,

you, as if our moon walker,
were brave and first.

Twinky Dancing

I go twinky dancing
On the edge of evening light,
Stilky leggéd quirky,
Prancing into night.

I go twinky dancing
As loony as a loon,
Crooning as I gallop
On lawns of twilight moon.

Morning Wash

I lick my hip
and with a flick
raise high my toe
above my nose,
incline my head
to spruce my neck
return your stare
with not a hair
smoothed out of place,
if you're amazed how's
this for that,
you're only human
I'm a cat.

Kitten Cat

Look at me a kitten cat,
Chase my tail and skitter cat.

Pretty cat, witty cat,
Stalk you where you're sitting cat.

Potty cat, dotty cat,
Dive into your shopping cat.

Kitty cat, skitty cat,
Rumple up your knitting cat.

Swinging cat, clinging cat,
Sing a little ditty cat.

Teasy cat, pleasy cat,
Rushing up the treesy cat.

Little cat, kitten cat,
Pitter pat, skitter scat,

Skitter scatter, scatter skitter,
Skitty kitty kitten cat.

Qu'elle est Belle   *for Nelle*

Tâches noires et blanches pattes,
'sait pas comment elle s'appelle
Une petite brave chatte.

Chivvied, chased, determined, spat,
Knows what kind of line to sell,
Tâches noires et blanches pattes.

Hunger squeezing belly flat
Instincts of survival swell,
Une petite brave chatte.

Spot a passing person that
Will listen to the tale she'll tell,
Tâches noires et blanches pattes.

Mewing plaintive diplomat
Finds a home to suit her well,
Une petite brave chatte.

She's purring a magnificat,
Approves we've called her 'Villanelle':
Tâches noires et blanches pattes,
Une petite brave chatte.

Who is Harris — What is She ?

The opinion is generally held
that
Harris is a cat.

But now and then some doubts
occur,
she doesn't purr.

Squattish, like the Sand Pit Fairy from
E. Nesbitt,
Harris could be definitely IT.

She rules her home with iron
paw,
no velvet hides her sharpened claw.

For she who'd starved and had it
tough,
decided that enough's enough.

Thirty litters leaves you
queasy,
time comes to move and take it easy.

Her tail, where tails most cats
enhance,
a crooked, broken, stricken lance.

Not well renowned for speed or
grace,
splattered smudges smite her face.

First, loving to her last born
small,
then hardly noticing at all

This son called
Tigger;
he is handsome, ginger, bigger.

Harris, saggy tortoiseshell and
white,
somehow looks all wrong but right.

For who would have her
otherwise?
Determination's yellow eyes

Fixed upon the people
whose
home and company she chose.

Wide whiskers sensitized
antennae
picking them from out of many

To keep her in the style she
knew
a Harris is entitled to:

Good food and for a Harris
nap
a comfortable and tweedy lap.

Relaxed and lazy, but she'd sometimes
rather
enjoy a little walk with father.

So is she, isn't she a
cat?
If not, then what? The question's that.

A funny sort of poem
this;
but what could you expect, for Harris?

Friend

When I want to be alone
I am glad of your company.
If I need to talk things through
your silence is advice.
Not offended by inanities,
no embarrassment at my caress,
the compliments I give
you gracefully receive;
your song of greeting lifts a flagging day.
Comfort exudes,
your relaxation permeates my work.
You doze in half-eyed watchful sleep,
make no demands,
take love for granted,
easy as throat's rhythms, shingle-rolled.

Vigil   *for Moses and Aaron*

Under the laburnum tree
the cat with blue eyes dreams alert,
his sadness and his cloud-cream coat
are warmed among white flowers.

And in this place
beneath the snow-in-summer,
cold and deep
in roots that breathe in nourishment,
his best companion sleeps
his blue eyes dulled;
he will not wake or suffer,
nor dream again
here in the sun among white flowers.

White as a Soul
for Maureen and Daisy May

An April day;
I work dark earth with roses
to carry colour's baton into summer.
I think of you, for
dainty, green-eyed as a snowdrop
she glides among the mid-spring flowers,
winds between the fluted daffodils.

The bells you placed
chink warning
to the birds you also loved;
all nature was your garden,
the merest slug unharmed.

Now, at home with me,
she curves her comforting across the lawn,
cat's paws on grass,
as clear and soft as secrets . . .
somewhere in my mind I hear your voice,
recall your feline smile,
the crinkled eyes,
and wish reality undone.

II

A white cat licks my hand,
You named her Daisy May,
I hope she understands;
You loved her when a stray.

I stroke her calm white fur,
Once on your lap she lay,
I feel her gentle purr,
You soothed all fear away.

She moves among my flowers,
Once by your pond she lazed,
Her green eyes light my hours,
On your sunned lawn she lazed.

She'd breathe with you today,
Her presence here unplanned,
You named her Daisy May,
A white cat licks my hand.

Not in the Cat Show

Me? I would not lower myself
to pose in some fancy-drape cage
for people to peer,
and worse
for some know-all person
to pick me up and criticise;
a suggestion that
my claws are unmanicured, my eye-colour pale,
my tail tip not perfectly rounded,
or pointed,
or whatever some ridiculous standard
says it should be.

I am a cat.
I am the way I like me.
I know where I look best.
I'll choose the place myself,
in my own time;
I can become invisibly elegant
on the white bedspread,
invisible but for my green (and perfect) eyes.
Or I will laze my length on the gold velvet sofa
which shows my limbs to sleek advantage.

I will not be deemed "nervous"
or "rather a lovely girl"
by passing judges.
I am a cat.
They cannot tell my grace and speed at climbing trees,
my skill and patience waiting for a mouse,
or how I know when the people I own have need of me.

I can be tender,
alluring,
always alert.
My night-time eyes are emeralds.
What do they know of my loud purr
when pleased or offering comfort?

Don't insult me with rosettes.
I know how good I am;
pretty damned-near perfect,
proud of it;
I am a cat.

Thought from the Goddess Bastet

Age is not be feared,
look at me my dear,
positively ancient;
beautiful, mysterious,
revered.

Papyrus

Papyrus the deep blue cat
sits in a mahogany frame,
still as still, unblinking,
till the London flat is quiet,
the people returned to the country.
Then she steps through the glass
her gold nose ring twinkling in celebration.

She stretches,
rolls kittenish on the carpet
and purrs the huge purr
of the worshipped.

How to Name Your Kitten

The naming of cats Mr Eliot taught
Is a delicate, intricate task.
For where to begin ? From whom to enquire ?
And what are the questions to ask ?

Should it be short, and easy to call,
Like Jasmine, or Florence, or Jade ?
Should it be subtle, with hints of mystique,
Like Whisper, or Isis, or Shade?

Perhaps you should trust in your power to invent,
Or resort to the Roman or Greek:
Phoebus, Apollo, Poseidon, Neptune,
Ribpurrer, Moonlover, or Sleek?

Then there are artists whose work you admire:
Luciano, Domingo, Rossini,
Olivier, Gielgud, or Miss Lapotaire,
Rembrandt, Matisse, or Bellini.

Slenderly slim as the Pharoahs esteemed,
Our kitten is half Abyssinian,
So Haile Selassie held high on the list,
But succumbed to the lilt of the Indian:-

For a stay in New Delhi preceded our pet,
And yielded Bawan, and Jantar,
Mahal and Mahatma, Quila and Masjid,
Gurdwara, Vigyan and Nagar.

We considered Yamuna, Jehan and Akbar,
We toyed with Lutyens from the Raj,
We floated Rajiv, Pradesh and Qutan,
But we finally settled on **TAJ.**

The kitten came home, and our son, seventeen,
Not noted for liking most cats,
Dissolved in a smile of love at first glance,
And said, "**TAJ!** You can't call him **THAT!**
He's **BERNARD.**"

And so he is.

Veterinary Visit

How can she do this to me?
'specially when I'm not well.
I have a cough
dark as the airing cupboard,
my throat like holly leaves
I could hardly nibble my breakfast.
But she pushes me, almost firmly,
into a dark trap of basket,
hard as sticks
with only a blanket for comfort,
bumps me on a roar of tin can wheels.
How unreasonable can you get ?
My stomach is a struggling mouse.

Then the room:
the smell of hygiene from a bottle,
the smell and sound of fear and dogs.
Silly voices saying it's all right.
All right for whom ?
the wittering dogs,
the squint-making light,
the man in green
with his claw-sharp needle ?

Ow! Now I *am* ill:
my dignity bruised.
Quick! The basket,
where I'll huddle safe, and sulk
through the bumping and roaring
till the lid opens,
twitch whiskers,
on my garden.

I escape - just in case,
try out a tree-top,
scrabble the reality of earth,
look at her over my shoulder,
purr, and wonder why
I feel a new cat.

175

Cherry Cat Pie   *for Bernard*

Magpie high in cherry tree
Cat upon the bough,
Magpie chatters teasingly
Cat's eyes glare and growl.

Magpie flies to branch below
Cat flings wild a paw,
Magpie cocky so-and-so,
Cat reviews his claws.

Magpie cheeks and jibes and jigs,
Cat plans cunning try,
Magpie thinks that cat's a pig,
Cat thinks cats might fly.

Magpie dances on his wits,
Cat glides sweet and neat,
Magpie rises, floats and flits,
Cat falls - on his feet.

Magpie up and smugly preens,
Cat has done what's done;
Magpie high in cherry tree,
Cat washes in the sun.

Picking the Chicken

Show me a chicken
fresh from the shops
tempting in wrapper,
deliciously raw.
I will claw
and eat it whole.

Carve me a chicken
hot from the oven
melting from bone,
hone me a slice:
hoicked in a trice
my instant pickings.

Leave me a chicken
cold on the plate,
leftovers labelled
"Help yourself"
on my personal shelf
and I'll say
"No thanks."

Ten Ways of Being a Great Help

N.B. Remember, helping is a skill. I am good at it, but it takes practice and may not be achieved lightly.

1. Sit in the middle of the letter she is writing, centre page spread, as this encourages lateral thinking.

2. Pound passionately over any book or pages she is studying, in case she is finding them boring.

3. Place your purring body exactly between her vision and the buttons she pushes on the telephone, enabling her to dial surprises.

4. Cheer the chore of unpacking the shopping, by exploring it for treats for you.

5. Never miss an opportunity to improve clothing with decorative patterns of hair.

6. Waltz determinedly on the worktops and all round her when she is dishing up a meal. This makes her believe her cooking is delicious.

7. Test the car alarm by leaping on the bonnet in the middle of the night, she needs to know how sensitive it is. If it fails to go off, your paw prints will show that you were trying.

8. Use your sixth sense to tell you when she's just sat down on the far side of a door, then give her some exercise by asking to come in.

9. Sit on the best furniture where it will give her pleasure to look at you.

10. **Never** let her be lonely, and when she is working and anxious for inspiration, unblock the word processor in one bound, writing

jaslfdkkjfnmerudkmgfkjwnkfndsa,flkaiownfm,ds

Which as everyone knows, means **I am a Great Help.**

Choice Bed

Ah! You've bought me a basket,
cat shaped wicker,
expensive with covers,
my bed - your choice.

I shall examine it,
give it a purr and a curl
for a day, maybe a week, but
choose and change place
as it suits:
my bed - my choice:

The warmth of the stair-top carpet,
a tower of towels in the linen cupboard,
a squash in a box - three sizes too small.

I shall perch on the breadbin,
top up an open drawer,
snuggle to Chopin on cassette.

I'll command an armchair,
extend on the sofa,
pound on your head in the night,
then provide you a challenge
round which to sleep your knees;
your bed - my choice.

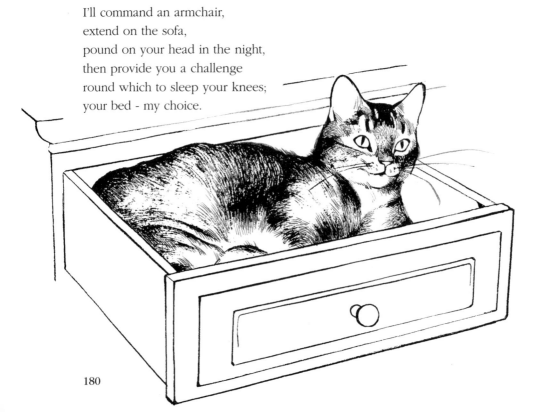

Love Scratch

Not being as retractile
as once he was,
Moses has caught his eye.

Favouring outdoors when fit,
he currently conspires
with the bedroom radiator
against the pain and cold.

Often aloof,
he now keeps close and quiet,
unresistant to the soothing cream
piped frequently
across the hurt pool of his eye,
accepts the weekly checkup;
vet's care
for "A nasty gash."

Healed,
he purrs against me
as I tend admin: on the desk,
gently he nibbles my hand
and deals me
an ecstatic pat.

Making his point
with tooth and paw,
but not being
as retractile
as once he was,
Moses writes
"Thank you"
in bright blood
upon my nose.

Moses in Montbretia

Moses in montbretia
hears her voice,
his name,
called and called
across the gardens.
He yawns,
stretches on warm leaves
under the wisteria wall.
Why worry ?
He's not hungry yet.

In the late summer heat
panic rises like steam.
Twenty-four hours have ticked;
not a sign
nor a note of a miaou.
Imagination stirs
the stomach pit,
snakes of anxiety
squirm and hiss
"Poisoned!"
"Snatched!"
"Older cat
heart attack!"

Word is spread,
neighbours check sheds
and undergrowth.
She calls his name,
his name
till three cats come,
but none of them is missing.

One dragged hour later
Moses in monbretia
under the wistaria wall
is found,
saucers blue-wide
to have occasioned worry.
Fluffed and sunny,
smug with the promise of fish,
he consents to be lifted home.

But why the fuss?
He knew where he was all the time.

Ern

Not for nothing am I called Big Ern,
I've learnt to work the system.
Twenty-two is old for a cat,
I wobble on bent pins,
my tail is frayed, well-used
as an ancient ironing flex.
With rusty miaou,
gaunt on slow limbs
I walk the long friend of our garden,
go through the hedge
to foreign lawns,
and commence the Stray's Doze:

With eyes slitted towards the house
I pose in the cold,
an obvious candidate for milk and meals.
Old and abandoned
I am suitably nervous;
flatter their knees with my warmth,
knowing that they like to care and worry,
this is my daily gift.

Later, I meander back,
safe as several houses,
rub against the no-place-like-home,
and purr to give her pleasure.
"Oh Ern," she says,
"You're just in time for supper."

The Old Cat

that
old cat
old flat cat
flat as a mat
furry old mat
furry old purry
purry old furry
furry old cuddly
cuddly old muddly
muddly old cuddly
cuddly old purry
purry old furry
furry old mat
flat as a mat
old flat cat
old cat
that

Thermometer

I know it is cold,
ice in the howl of night,
the clench of frost on air.

I can tell it bites
by the fur I'm wearing
deep in my igloo bed.

The prowl of night abandoned,
he favours a cave of covers,
warmth to warmth

he purrs
in the curve
of my sleeping.

The Bedtime Milk   *for Silvester*

I like milk;
its cool smoothness
calms as it plips,
plip, plip, against
the rough warmth
of my tongue.

I like milk
from the yellow dish,
full to its
daily plastic rim;
ours to share
in routine plunder,
filling our thirst.

But bedtime milk
is served upstairs
in a cut glass dish
afloat on deep carpet;
a prelude to sleep,
sharing their bed,
their night.

Milk,
a potion for dreams
or secret wish,
all for me,
a creamy silk
tasting of
moonlight.

The Cats Ride Out

When the moon is wide
And the wind is long
And the stars are on your side,
It is then in the blue
Of the night-time grue
That the cats come out to ride.

There's a toss of mist
And the hoof beats strong
As they garner to their tryst,
There's the caterwaul
Of the green-eyed call
In the making of the list...

Circe smooth on Milkyway
And Trim on Flying Free,
Grimelda high on Dancing Proud
And Tegg on Cherokee,
Siegfried light on Rivendell,
With Seth on Floating Cream,
Hippolyta is safe on Spell,
And Jake on Waking Dream.

In the trembled height
Of the cantered sky
Their eyes are the gems of night;
In the shadowed dark
There's the cold of spark,
And a breath of "may" or "might".

189

In the haunt of dawn
When the birds are song
And the horses' ways are worn,
There's the doze of day
In the clowdered hay,
And the purr of fur on yawn.